Reading Skills
For Adults
Blue Book

Laurence Swinburne

John F. Warner

Steck-Vaughn Adult Education Advisory Council

STECK-VAUGHN COMPANY
AUSTIN, TEXAS
A Division of National Education Corporation

About the Authors

LAURENCE SWINBURNE is a widely published author of children's reading materials. His works include numerous books, short stories, and filmstrips. He is the author or coauthor of several reading programs, both basal and supplementary. Mr. Swinburne is a graduate of Princeton University, where he majored in English. He received a master's degree in education from Rutgers University. He is a former textbook editor and publishing executive, and is currently the president of the Swinburne Readability Laboratory. He is a member of the National Council of Teachers of English, the International Reading Association, and Kappa Delta Phi.

JOHN F. WARNER has been involved in education, as a teacher and administrator, and in publishing, as a writer, editor, and consultant, for more than twenty years. He has taught in elementary, junior and senior high schools as well as adult levels. His published works include studies of English and American literature, short stories, several supplementary reading programs, and more than one hundred articles in professional journals, magazines, and newspapers. Mr. Warner is a member of the International Reading Association and the National Council of Teachers of English. He received his B.S. and A.M. degrees from Clark University.

Reading Skills for Adults Series
Blue Book
Red Book
Green Book
Brown Book

Cover photo by Tomás Pantin

NOTICE: Answer Key is bound in the back of the book on perforated pages.

ISBN 0-8114-1617-8

1 2 3 4 5 6 7 8 9 0 HG 90 89 88 87 86

CONTENTS

THE RIVALS

Hal and Red had never gotten along. They had been rivals ever since high school. Now they were in the same army company. Would they be able to work with each other? Or would there be trouble?

Globe Photos

WORDS YOU SHOULD KNOW

Study these words and their meanings before you read the story.

basic training—training given to soldiers in the army
- He learned to use his rifle in **basic training**.

paratrooper—a soldier trained to jump from planes using a parachute
- The **paratrooper** hit the ground and then got out of his parachute.

sergeant—a military officer who often trains new soldiers
- The **sergeant** ordered her company to line up.

grenade—a small bomb that explodes when thrown
- He threw the **grenade** and it exploded.

graduation—an event for people who passed classes in a school
- My mother came to my **graduation** from army basic training.

obstacle—something in the way that must be overcome
- The biggest **obstacle** between graduation and me is passing history.

1

Dear Joe,

I'm sorry I haven't dropped you a line before. Basic training is sure keeping me busy! It's hard to find any free time.

I thought I was ready for anything when I got here. What I was not ready for was Red Burke. You remember. He was the big champ at East High. Every time we played East High, it was Red Burke who killed us. No one in our school could stand him.

Now, of all the bad luck, Red Burke is in my company. He sleeps in the bunk next to me. He marches next to me too. Can you beat that? In this big army I have to get stuck next to the one guy who really ticks me off!

Wish I could say I was happy. Write soon.

Hal

Wide World/AP Photos

Dear Joe,

Thanks for the letter. It made my day. You are right about one thing—I am really getting in shape. Basic training does that for you.

You asked about Burke. No, we are not getting along. I have made up my mind to show him up. I'm going to beat him in everything. He thinks he was a football champ at East High, but I'll show him who is a champ in the army.

Today, I beat him on the obstacle course. You know, going over walls, hanging on ropes, climbing, and things like that. It felt good.

He beat me on the firing range. I got the Sharpshooter's Badge. That's very good. But he made Expert. I have to say he's a better shot—so far.

I threw a grenade much further than Burke did. The sergeant said that was good. Then he said, "Williams, it would also be good to hit the target." How I burned! Burke hit the target with his grenade.

It's not easy to be a champ.

Your tired friend,

Hal

2

Dear Joe,

This week we had night training. I was doing fine until I fell into quicksand. What a feeling! I had all this heavy gear on and I was sinking. I was scared, believe me. Then, who comes along and pulls me out just as I was going under? Burke! I was so mad, I didn't even thank him.

As for him, all he said was, "If I had known it was you, I would have gone on."

I think the sergeant has been watching Burke and me during basic. Last night, he put boxing gloves on the two of us. "You can fight it out," he said.

Well, we knocked each other around for five minutes. Then, we stopped. We were too tired, you see. Night training had done us in.

Suddenly, I started to laugh. I couldn't help it! Burke did too. The whole thing just seemed so silly. Maybe basic training is bigger than both of us.

Best,

Hal

Dear Joe,

Well, yesterday was graduation. We got our papers to show us where we go next. I got paratroopers—just what I asked for!

Burke came over while I was looking at my papers. "Where are you going?" he asked.

"Fort Benning," I said. "Paratroopers."

He grinned. "Me too. See you there."

Suddenly, I felt good about that. In a way, our being rivals had helped us both do better in basic training. I think that at Fort Benning we might even be friends.

So that's the way it is, old pal. I'll drop you a line from Benning.

Pfc Williams

APPLYING
READING
SKILLS

A. FINDING THE MAIN IDEA

The main idea of a story is what the story is mainly about.

Put a check (✓) before the sentence that best tells what this story is about.

.... 1. Army basic training is hard work.

.... 2. Army life makes people mean.

.... 3. Even rivals can become friends once they get to know each other.

.... 4. Football and army basic training are very much alike.

B. RECALLING DETAILS

Draw a line under the best ending for each sentence.

1. The person who tells the story is
   a. Red Burke.
   b. Hal Williams.
   c. Joe.

2. Red Burke played football for
   a. West High.
   b. the army.
   c. East High.

3. Hal and Red first became rivals when they
   a. played football in high school.
   b. went into the army.
   c. graduated from basic training.

4. In basic training Hal wanted <u>most</u> to
   a. be voted best soldier.
   b. play football for the army post team.
   c. show up Red Burke.

5. Hal and Red became friends
   a. during high school.
   b. at Fort Benning.
   c. during basic training.

C. IDENTIFYING SYNONYMS

Words that have the same, or nearly the same, meaning are called *synonyms*. *Grin* and *smile* are synonyms, as are *stop* and *halt*.

On each blank write another word you might use in place of the underlined word. Choose from these words.

disliked   bed   weary   afraid   completed

.... 1. I was too <u>tired</u>.

.... 2. Now basic training is <u>finished</u>.

.... 3. Remember how the two of us <u>hated</u> each other?

.... 4. There he was ... in the next <u>bunk</u>!

.... 5. I was <u>scared</u> to look at my papers.

D. IDENTIFYING ANTONYMS

An *antonym* is a word that is opposite in meaning to another word. *Weak* and *strong*, *light* and *heavy*, and *calm* and *nervous* are pairs of antonyms.

Put a check (✓) before each pair of antonyms.

.... 1. great, small   .... 2. championship, title

.... 3. die, live   .... 4. together, apart

.... 5. like, care for   .... 6. march, parade

.... 7. remember, forget   .... 8. laugh, chuckle

.... 9. dirty, foul   .... 10. pal, buddy

THE POWER OF SONG

Prison life is hard. You need friends there. The Dummy didn't have any . . . until she picked up a guitar.

Susan Jane Stone

WORDS YOU SHOULD KNOW
Study these words and their meanings before you read the story.

softball—a baseball game, played with a larger ball
  • She hit two home runs in the **softball** game.

chaplain—religious leader in a prison, hospital, or other large group
  • The **chaplain** helped us form a self-help club.

village—a small town
  • Everyone in the **village** knew one another.

band—a group of musicians
  • The five-piece **band** played rock music.

guitar—a musical instrument with strings
  • Willie Nelson sure can pluck a **guitar**.

In prison you get to know people pretty well. You talk a lot. You talk about where you come from. You talk about how you got to be behind bars.

But the new woman was different. She didn't talk at all. That's why we called her The Dummy. Just like a dummy in a store window. Quiet as a mouse! She cried at night, though. I could hear her.

The other women didn't like her.

"I think she's stuck-up," said Flora. "She thinks she's too good for the rest of us."

"Yeah, that's why she won't talk to us," said Tina.

"Aw, come on!" I said. "The kid is just shy."

The chaplain talked to me one day. He said, "Rose, you're a leader around here. Help the kid, will you?"

Well, I tried. I got The Dummy into the painting class. She dropped paint all over the place, but not on her picture. I got her to go out for the softball team. She dropped more balls than she did paint.

"Get her out of here before the team kills her," said Joan.

The Dummy just didn't fit in. The other women made fun of her. Things got worse and worse. The Dummy looked sadder and sadder.

Then a band came to play at the prison. The Five Foxes was what they called themselves. They were OK. Not great, just OK. But The Dummy loved them. She jumped up and down while the band played. She clapped and yelled after each number. It was like watching a dead thing come alive!

The band finished playing. They hung around to talk with us. At first, no one saw The Dummy pick up the band's guitar. At first, no one even heard her playing it.

Then The Dummy began to sing. She sang about the hills around her home. She sang about the summer and the winter there. She sang about rivers and trees. She sang about her children. The Dummy's song was all about what she loved and missed.

Powers/Frost Publishing Group

The Dummy stopped singing. She kept playing the guitar, though.

Then, Flora began to sing. She sang about her home. It was in a village by the sea. Flora sang about the wind and the waves. She sang about the children she left behind.

After that, each of us took a turn. I sang about the noisy

7

city I missed so much. Joan sang about her mom and dad. Tina sang about her kids sitting in her lap.

The Dummy kept playing that guitar. And we kept singing.

Finally, one of the Foxes said to The Dummy, "Hey, you're real good. You play a mean guitar! What's your name?"

"Sara," said The Dummy. "My name is Sara."

The Foxes packed up and began to leave. We couldn't leave. The bars held us in. All we had was each other.

We all stood around The Dummy. But she wasn't The Dummy anymore. She was Sara. And Sara was smiling at last. The rest of us were, too.

Music had made something magic happen. Sara's song brought us closer together. We shared so much, because we had all lost so much. Sara helped us to see that. She was part of us now.

David E. Kennedy/Texastock

APPLYING
READING
SKILLS

A. FINDING THE MAIN IDEA

Sometimes the main idea of a story can be shown in its title. Here are four other titles for the story about women in prison.

Put a check (✓) before the one that best tells what the story is mainly about.

.... 1. Women in Prison

.... 2. The Five Foxes

.... 3. The Music Lesson

.... 4. Prisoners Have Feelings, Too

B. RECALLING DETAILS

Read each sentence below. Write _true_ if the sentence is true according to the story. Write _false_ if the sentence is not true.

.... 1. The person who tells the story is named Rose.

.... 2. Rose, Joan, and their friends form a band they call the Five Foxes.

.... 3. Most of the prisoners were from hill country towns.

.... 4. The leader of the prisoners was Joan.

.... 5. Rose thought the band sounded great.

.... 6. At first The Dummy did not fit in well with the other prisoners.

.... 7. The Dummy knew how to play a guitar.

.... 8. Each of the prisoners sang a song about her home.

.... 9. Joan thought of having the Five Foxes record their song.

.... 10. The women prisoners gave the money they earned from their song to The Dummy.

.... 11. Sara lived in a noisy city.

.... 12. Music helped the women prisoners share their feelings.

C. IDENTIFYING SYNONYMS

Write a synonym for each word below. Choose from the following list of words.

bashful	perform	remain	ladies
quick	quiet	untamed	ocean
began	pleasant	poor	song
unusual	watching	unhappy	shouted

1. started ....

2. stay ....

3. play ....

4. shy ....

5. broke ....

6. women ....

7. wild ....

8. sudden ....

9. sea ....

10. nice ....

11. silence ....

12. tune ....

13. different ....

14. looking ....

15. yelled ....

16. sad ....

D. IDENTIFYING ANTONYMS

Put a check (✓) before each pair of antonyms.

.... 1. going, coming

.... 2. radio, TV

.... 3. sang, talked

.... 4. make, lose

.... 5. summer, fall

.... 6. jump, leap

.... 7. stopped, ceased

.... 8. shy, talkative

.... 9. finished, started

.... 10. dropped, caught

.... 11. walking, running

.... 12. yell, whisper

.... 13. silence, noise

.... 14. badly, poorly

.... 15. play, rest

.... 16. well, good

.... 17. dead, alive

.... 18. country, farm

10

MAN WITH A DREAM

Walter had a dream. He wanted to draw cartoons. It wasn't an easy way to make a living. But Walter got help from a mouse.

Wide World/AP Photos

WORDS YOU SHOULD KNOW
Study these words and their meanings before you read the story.

cartoon—a funny picture
- My favorite **cartoon** is *Peanuts.*

deliver—hand over
- Postal workers **deliver** mail.

drawing—a picture done with a pencil, pen, or crayon
- Most comic strips are **drawings**.

legal—lawful
- A driver's license is a **legal** paper.

office—a place where work is done
- My sister's law **office** is downtown.

success—the result that was hoped for
- **Success** usually comes to those who work hard.

11

Walter's family was very poor. They could not make a living from their farm. They sold the land and moved to the city. But life was still hard.

Every person in the family had to help. Walter had to get up each morning at 3:30. Then he went out to deliver newspapers before school.

As he got older, he worked at many jobs. He sold candy on trains. He worked in a jelly plant with his father. He also worked in a post office.

He had to give all the money he made to his father. Even in World War I, he sent home all the money he made when he was in Europe.

Walter had a dream. He wanted to become a cartoonist. He took lessons in drawing. But his father was against this. He wanted Walter to go on working with him.

Walter left home. He went to Kansas City, Missouri. He started drawing ads for newspapers. But he could not make much money.

In 1923 he went to California. He was 21 years old. Movies were very new then. Walter began to make cartoon movies.

For the first time, Walter found success. He didn't make a lot of money. But he made enough to marry.

One of his best cartoons was about Oswald the Lucky Rabbit. All over the country, people loved the funny animal.

Walt Disney loved trains. This is the locomotive he had built at Disneyland.

A company in New York would sell the cartoon movies about Oswald to movie houses. They would send part of the money they got to Walter.

Walter did not think that he was getting enough money for Oswald. He and his wife went to New York. Charles Mintz, the head of the company, laughed at Walter.

"From now on, I will pay you less," said Mintz.

Walter became angry. "Then you will get no more Oswalds," he said.

"Yes, I will," said Mintz. "I own Oswald."

He showed Walter a legal paper. It said Mintz owned Oswald. There was nothing Walter could do. He had never made a legal claim showing he had thought up Oswald.

"Then I won't send you any more Oswalds," Walter said.

Wide World Photos

"I don't care," said Mintz. "Four of the cartoonists who work for you are coming to work for me. They will do more Oswalds for me."

On the way back to California, Walter was still angry. "I will never work for anyone else," he told his wife. "I have to think up another cartoon." He took out a piece of paper and a pen.

He remembered that a mouse had made its home in his office in Kansas City. Walter and the mouse had become friends.

"How do you like this?" he called to his wife. He showed her a picture of the mouse.

She laughed. "I like him. He looks funny with clothes on. What did you call him?"

"Mortimer."

She made a face. "That's not a good name for him."

Walter thought for a while. "How about Mickey? Mickey Mouse!"

And that was the way Mickey Mouse was born.

What about Walter, the boy with a dream? Not many people knew him as Walter. They called him "Walt"—Walt Disney!

Brown Brothers

Walt Disney had many dreams. And most of them came true. He didn't stop with Mickey Mouse. He also created Donald Duck, Pluto, Goofy, and more.

Walt died in 1966. But his dreams live on. They live in Disneyland in California. And in Walt Disney World in Florida. They also live in the many movies he left us.

APPLYING
READING
SKILLS

A. RECALLING DETAILS

Draw a line under the best ending for each sentence.

1. This is a
   a. true story.
   b. fable.
   c. legend.

2. Walt Disney's dream was to become a
   a. famous moviemaker.
   b. rich man.
   c. cartoonist.

3. As a young boy, Walt lived
   a. in New York City.
   b. on a farm.
   c. in Europe.

4. Walt's father wanted his son to
   a. work with him.
   b. be a cartoonist.
   c. earn a lot of money.

5. One of Walt's first films was about
   a. Mintz Mouse.
   b. Oswald the Lucky Rabbit.
   c. Mickey Mouse.

6. Walt first named Mickey Mouse
   a. Mortimer.
   b. Mintz.
   c. Morgan.

7. When Walt made his movies, he lived in
   a. California.
   b. New York City.
   c. Europe.

B. FINDING THE MAIN IDEA

The *main idea* of a story is what the story is mainly about.

Put a check (✓) before the sentence that best tells what this story is about.

.... 1. Few people can be trusted.

.... 2. Work hard and your dreams may come true.

.... 3. To succeed, you must be your own boss.

.... 4. Life is harder for poor people than it is for rich people.

Read this paragraph. Decide what the paragraph is mostly about. Circle the letter of each answer that is true below.

> He showed Walter a legal paper. It said Mintz owned Oswald.
> There was nothing Walter could do. He had never made a legal claim showing he had thought up Oswald.

1. The paragraph above is mainly about
   a. Oswald.
   b. Charles Mintz.
   c. a legal paper.

2. What is the meaning of the word *claim* as it is used in the last sentence of the paragraph?
   a. the right to a piece of land
   b. a right to something someone else has

C. IDENTIFYING SYNONYMS

On each blank write another word you might use in place of the underlined word. Choose from these words.

| training | began | difficult | goal | have |

.... 1. Walter had a <u>dream</u>.

.... 2. I <u>own</u> Oswald.

.... 3. Walter took <u>lessons</u> in drawing.

.... 4. Living in the city was <u>hard</u>.

.... 5. He <u>started</u> drawing ads for newspapers.

15

SKIPPER

Beverly Kelley did not like her job at the bank. She hated sitting behind a desk all day. She decided to join the Coast Guard. But after she got in, she wondered if she had only exchanged one desk for another.

Official U.S. Coast Guard Photo

WORDS YOU SHOULD KNOW
Study these words and their meanings before you read the story.

command—have power over
- The captain was in **command** of her ship.

crew—people who do the work on a ship
- Every ship needs a good **crew**.

future—what is to come
- Do you ever wonder what the **future** holds for you?

insult—treat with rudeness
- She **insulted** her friend by not listening.

officer—person who commands others in the armed forces
- My brother was a navy **officer** during World War II.

polite—showing good manners
- Everyone likes **polite** people.

"Working in a bank is a good job for many people," Beverly Kelley thought. "But not for me."

She looked around the bank from her desk. "What's wrong with me?" she wondered. "I am liked here. I have a fine future in this work. But I find it dull, dull, dull. I just don't like being tied down to a desk."

Beverly Kelley knew what she did like to do. She liked being out in a boat. There was nothing like a good sea wind and the feeling of water in your face.

She had been brought up in Miami, the city on the water. When she was younger, she had worked on boats.

But there was no real future for her on boats. Or was there? She saw a notice about the United States Coast Guard. There were openings for both men and women.

Should she join the Coast Guard? She looked around the bank and shook her head. Then she looked out of the window and saw the ocean. That was when she made up her mind.

After signing up with the Coast Guard, Beverly Kelley found the work she had done on boats came to good use. She was sent to a special school. When she finished, she was an officer. "Now," she thought, "I will go to sea."

But, no, that was not to be. Each of her classmates—all men—went out on ships. As for Beverly, she found herself in a place she had been before—on land and behind a desk.

Courtesy United States Coast Guard

Courtesy United States Coast Guard

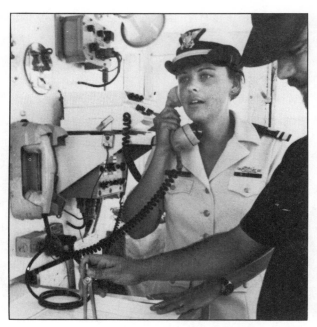

Beverly Kelley decided to fight to go to sea. She sent many letters to Coast Guard headquarters in Washington, D.C. The letters were polite, but she told them how she felt. She asked if she was going to be stationed on land forever. That was not why she had joined.

In the past, Coast Guard women had not gone to sea. But times were changing. And Beverly Kelley was one of the women who brought about the changes.

Finally, she got a letter from Washington. "You are shipping out on the *Morgenthau*," it said. She was going to sea at last!

Her new work was not easy, though. Her ship patrolled the waters off Alaska. She was given the job of navigator—figuring out the course of the ship. Later, she became gunnery officer. That is, she directed the shooting of the ship's guns.

It was all very new to her. The hardest part was when she made a mistake. Sometimes the mistake was blamed on her being a woman. It hurt. But she had made up her mind to win out, and she did.

Then she got her big break. Her work on the *Morgenthau* was so good, she was picked out of almost 100 officers to command a ship of her own. It was named the *Cape Newagen*.

She took over her ship in Hawaii. Her crew was made up of 14 men. Half of them were older than she. That was why she got a kick out of being called "The Old Lady." It was not an insult. It showed she was accepted for what she was—a good skipper. You see, a male captain is usually called "The Old Man."

APPLYING
READING
SKILLS

A. RECALLING DETAILS

Draw a line under the best ending for each sentence.

1. Before she joined the Coast Guard, Beverly Kelley worked as a
   a. schoolteacher.
   b. sailing instructor.
   c. bank clerk.

2. Beverly grew up in
   a. Miami, Florida.
   b. Washington, D.C.
   c. Honolulu, Hawaii.

3. Beverly decided to join the Coast Guard
   a. because she was bored with her job.
   b. in order to go to college.
   c. so she could travel the world.

4. Once in the Coast Guard, Beverly
   a. was pleased with the work she had to do.
   b. found that the work she was doing was a lot like the work she had wanted to get away from.
   c. said she made a mistake in joining.

5. Beverly wrote many letters to get the kind of job she wanted. That showed she was
   a. determined.
   b. afraid.
   c. angry.

6. The *Morgenthau* was
   a. a city in Alaska.
   b. the name of a ship.
   c. Beverly's name before she got married.

B. FINDING THE MAIN IDEA

Circle the number of the phrase that best tells what this story is about.

1. Beverly Kelley
2. the United States Coast Guard
3. jobs
4. women in the armed forces

C. DEFINING WORDS

Match each word to its meaning in the story.

.... 1. wonder   a. printed sign

.... 2. notice   b. hold responsible

.... 3. special   c. sailing to find information

.... 4. station   d. wish to know

.... 5. patrol   e. take what is offered

.... 6. navigator   f. different from others

.... 7. blame   g. person who tells where a ship should go

.... 8. accept   h. place where sailors work

D. USING CONTEXT CLUES

Fill in the blanks in this paragraph. Choose from the words below. Use each word only once.

command   writing   ship
determination   desk   woman

The Coast Guard gave Beverly Kelley a .... job because she was

a .... She began .... to Coast Guard headquarters, asking

to go to sea. Her .... paid off. She finally gained .... of

a .... called the *Cape Newagen*.

SUPERSTAR

He is almost forgotten today. But in his time, he was a star in three sports. He played football and baseball and ran track. Some people say he was the greatest sports star of all time. His name was Jim Thorpe.

Western History Collection/University of Oklahoma Library

WORDS YOU SHOULD KNOW

Study these words and their meanings before you read the story.

coach—teacher
- A good **coach** can teach a person how to play a sport better.

league—a group of sports teams
- Melinda thinks the Giants are the best team in the National **League**.

Native American—native-born Indian
- Sitting Bull was a **Native American**.

penalty—punishment
- For tripping another skater, the hockey player was given a **penalty**.

professional—person who plays a sport for money
- Martina Navratilova is a **professional** tennis player.

sportswriter—person who writes about sports in newspapers
- A **sportswriter** covered the game.

touchdown—score made in a football game
- A team gets six points for every **touchdown** it scores.

Who is the greatest sports star of all time? Earl Campbell? Martina Navratilova? Julius Irving? Carl Lewis?

All of these are tops in their games. But when sportswriters are asked, they pick a Native American whose name is not often remembered today.

He belonged to the Sauk and Fox tribe. His Indian name was Wa-Tho-Huck. That means Bright Path. It was a good name for him. He was to make many bright paths through football teams. He also had another name—Jim Thorpe.

No one had heard of him when he came from Oklahoma to the Carlisle Indian Industrial School in Pennsylvania. He had not come to play games. He had come to learn how to make clothes.

One of the school's football coaches saw Thorpe play in a pickup game. He could hardly believe how fast the young man could run. Right then and there, he asked Jim to be on the football team.

Carlisle was a small school. But it played some of the best teams in the country. When it met Harvard in 1911, Harvard had not lost a game. It was thought that Carlisle would be lucky if it could hold the other team to 50 points.

Culver Pictures

But at the half, Carlisle was leading 9–6. That was because Jim Thorpe had drop-kicked three field goals. To drop-kick, he dropped the ball on its end to the ground. He kicked it just as the ball hit the ground. This was much harder than the place-kick players do today.

In the second half, Harvard went ahead 15–9. But then Thorpe tied the game with his hard running. At the last second he kicked a 50-yard field goal to win!

In the 1912 game against Army, Jim took a kickoff. He went 90 yards through the whole Army team for a touchdown. But one of the Carlisle players had made a penalty. The touchdown didn't count. Army kicked off again. And this time Thorpe ran 95 yards for a score. He laughed about it later. "That's the longest run I ever made," he said. "I had to run 185 yards to make just one touchdown."

The Harvard and Army games were his best two games. But when he was playing, Carlisle hardly ever lost. He could do almost anything with the ball. Once he punted 90 yards. His longest dropkick was 79 yards!

Football was not his only game. He was also one of the best track stars of all time. Once, he and four other Native

United Press International

Culver Pictures

Jim Thorpe was an outstanding football player. He could run, block, tackle, and kick. In his last year at Carlisle, he made 25 touchdowns and scored 198 points. In 1951 he was one of the first players admitted to the National Football Foundation's Hall of Fame.

Thorpe was the first athlete to win both the pentathlon and decathlon. He did it at the 1912 Olympic Games. He is shown here throwing the javelin.

Americans made up the whole track team. They went to Lafayette College for a meet. The Lafayette coach could not believe his eyes when he saw only five Indians.

"You have to be joking," he said to the Carlisle coach. "We have 45 men on our team."

The Carlisle coach was watching Jim warm up. "I don't need any more," he said. "Come to think of it, maybe I need only one."

That day Jim won five events. He finished second in the 100-yard dash. He was a little tired by that time, he said.

But he could do even better. Against Harvard he entered eight events. He was first in all of them!

The Bettmann Archive

He was picked for the 1912 Olympic Games. He entered the decathlon and pentathlon. In these he had to do a number of events. Of course, he won both. No one since has been able to do that.

A few weeks later, his medals were taken away. Before the Olympics he had played baseball for a small amount of money. That made him a professional. Pros are not allowed to enter the Olympics.

After he finished Carlisle, he played both professional baseball and football.

He was not a star in baseball. But he was good enough to play in the big leagues. He was also good at bowling, boxing, and swimming. With his quick hands and sure eyes, he might have become a star basketball player. But basketball was not the big game it is today. So he never tried it.

Jim Thorpe died in 1953. Many people have forgotten him. And many have never heard of him. But those who know his records say that Jim Thorpe—Wa-Tho-Huck—was the greatest of them all.

APPLYING READING SKILLS

A. RECALLING DETAILS

Read each sentence below. Write *true* if the sentence is true according to the story. Write *false* if the sentence is not true.

.... 1. The story says that Jim Thorpe was the best sports star of all time.

.... 2. Wa-Tho-Huck is another name for Carl Lewis.

.... 3. Carlisle was an Indian school in Oklahoma.

.... 4. Jim Thorpe said his longest touchdown run was 185 yards.

.... 5. Of all the sports he played, Jim Thorpe was best at baseball.

.... 6. Jim Thorpe never tried to play basketball.

.... 7. Jim Thorpe was an Olympic star.

.... 8. Jim Thorpe's best football games were against Army and Lafayette.

.... 9. Jim Thorpe went to school to learn how to run machines.

.... 10. Jim Thorpe died in 1953.

B. RECOGNIZING COMPOUND WORDS

When two words are joined, the new word is called a *compound word*. For example, *out* and *side* can be joined to form the compound *outside*.

Some of the words below are compound words. Some are not. If a word is a compound word, write the two words that make it up. Do not write anything if a word is not a compound word.

1. sportswriter ....

2. touchdown ....

3. professional ....

4. football ....

5. pickup ....

6. dropkick ....

7. native ....

8. baseball ....

9. medals ....

10. basketball ....

11. record ....

12. kickoff ....

C. UNDERSTANDING ROOT WORDS

A *root* is a base word that endings are added to. The word *class* is the root of words like *classy*, *classmate*, and *classify*.

For each word, write its root in the blank given.

1. twisted ....

2. ruined ....

3. believed ....

4. turned ....

5. submarine ....

6. palaces ....

7. forgotten ....

8. nearer ....

9. golden ....

10. poured ....

11. roared ....

12. buildings ....

13. swimming ....

14. greatest ....

WHEELCHAIR RUNNER

The marathon judges had never heard of anyone "running" in a wheelchair. The 26-mile race was a real killer. They didn't think someone who couldn't walk would be able to make it. But they didn't know how wrong they were.

David Wharton

WORDS YOU SHOULD KNOW

Study these words and their meanings before you read the story.

ache—a steady pain
  • If I chop firewood on Saturday, my arms will **ache** for two days.

judge—a person who decides the winner of a race or contest
  • Important footraces have several **judges** to be sure that the right winner is picked.

marathon—a long footrace, usually 26 miles and 385 yards
  • Each year thousands of people run in the Boston **Marathon**.

post—a distance marker
  • Marathons usually have **posts** so that the runners can tell how far they have to go to reach the finish line.

My brother, Martin, is one tough person. One day about three years ago, he was playing stickball. A car came tearing around the corner and hit him. It threw him across the street.

You might think Martin is lucky to be alive. My mother and father were at the hospital for two straight days, not knowing if he would pull through. He made it by an inch. But he could not use his legs anymore. Martin would be in a wheelchair for the rest of his life.

David Wharton

That would be hard on any person. But it was ten times as hard on Martin. He loved sports. At North Junior High School, he had been a star in soccer, basketball, and baseball.

I thought Martin would never get used to the wheelchair. I do not think I would. For months he hardly would speak to anyone. He wouldn't even go out of the house.

Then one day Martin changed. I do not know why. He learned how to play stickball in a wheelchair. That sounds crazy, but it is true. Martin became good at it, too.

He would even take long "walks" around the city. Sometimes, I would walk with him, but I never finished. I would get tired trying to keep up with him.

Last spring he told me that he was going to enter the city marathon. I tried to talk him out of it. I was afraid people would laugh at him. But nothing I said could change his mind.

"Let them laugh," Martin said. "What do I care?"

"Twenty-six miles is a very long way." I said.

"It sure is, Sharon," he answered, grinning.

Martin trained hard for the race. Then the day of the race finally arrived. We drove Martin down to the starting point. The judges of the race said he could not enter. "But I have entered," he said, "I paid by mail. You sent me this letter saying I was in the race."

"But you did not tell us you were in a wheelchair," they said.

Well, the other runners yelled at the judges to let Martin race. They sure made a lot of noise about it.

At last, the chief judge held his hands over his ears. "All right," he said. "He can race. Only we will give him a fifteen-minute head start."

Off Martin wheeled. Fifteen minutes later, the rest of the runners began.

Nobody thought Martin would last too long. I did not think

so, either. I rode my bike out to the five-mile post. I thought he would stop there. But he came by me as strong as ever.

The same thing happened at the ten-mile post. He grinned and waved at me as he went by.

When Martin got to the twenty-mile post, I began to believe he could do it. Other runners had passed him, but not too many.

I followed him the rest of the way. The last two miles are straight uphill. A lot of runners never make it.

Martin looked very tired by this time. But he would not give up. His arms must have been aching, but they kept on pushing the wheels of that heavy wheelchair.

Then he went past the finish line. You never heard such cheers. People ran up to him. They patted his back and shook his hand.

Martin did not win. But he was number twenty out of two hundred.

"Of course he really was not *in* the race," said a judge. "We cannot give him any prize."

Martin did not care. He was just trying to show he could do it.

He is going to be in the marathon again next spring. He will not be alone this time. More than twenty wheelchair people have said they will be in the race, too. The judges are going to give prizes to the wheelchair runners this time.

I just wish I were half as strong as Martin.

David Wharton

APPLYING
READING
SKILLS

A. DEFINING WORDS

Write the letter of the best meaning before each word.

.... 1. wheelchair   a. hurting

.... 2. hospital   b. a very long race

.... 3. judge   c. active games taken up for exercise, pleasure, or pay

.... 4. marathon   d. a seat that rolls

.... 5. cheers   e. a place where sick people are helped

.... 6. sports   f. shouts of joy

.... 7. alive   g. a person who has been picked to tell who wins

.... 8. aching   h. not dead

B. FINDING THE MAIN IDEA

Circle the number of the phrase that tells what this story is mainly about.

1. an auto accident   2. Martin

3. unfair judges   4. wheelchairs

C. DRAWING CONCLUSIONS

Finish each sentence by writing what you think is the best answer.

1. Martin has a physical disability. The word *disability* means

----

2. The person who tells the story likes Martin because

----

3. Martin's sister tries to keep him out of the marathon because

----

4. The judges finally let Martin race because

D. USING CONTEXT CLUES

Fill in the blanks in this paragraph. Choose from the words below. Use each word only once.

| finished | wheelchair | yelled | accident |
| marathon | star | training | judges |

Martin was a .... in soccer, basketball, and baseball. Then he was

injured in an automobile .... He had to use a .... to get

around. But Martin could not give up being a sports star. He began ....

for the city .... At first, the .... would not let a person

in a wheelchair run the marathon. But the other runners .... until the

judges changed their minds. Martin .... the race, number 20 in a field
of 200.

E. SUMMARIZING A STORY

A *summary* is a short statement giving the main points of a story. The paragraph in exercise D is an example of a summary.

Write a summary of "Wheelchair Runner" in your own words. First, reread the story and look for important facts. Then write a short summary (three or four sentences).

....

....

....

....

....

....

....

....

....

....

....

THE OLYMPIC SPIRIT

Adolf Hitler hated the black athlete. How could he stop the young American from winning in the Olympics? One of the Olympic judges would try— and succeed for a while.

Bettmann Archives

WORDS YOU SHOULD KNOW

Study these words and their meanings before you read the story.

stadium—an egg-shaped or U-shaped building, open in the center where sports are played
  • The football **stadium** can hold lots of people.

dictator—a ruler who has complete power over his country
  • Hitler was the **dictator** of Germany.

athlete—a person who plays a sport
  • Who are the best **athletes** in football, baseball, soccer, and tennis?

Olympics—sports games like those held in ancient Greece
  • The **Olympics** are held every four years in a different country.

qualify—to pass a test; to prove one is fit to do a certain task
  • Did he **qualify** to take the driving test?

spirit—a way of thinking and feeling
  • I like the crowd's **spirit** when they sing "America."

The stadium in Berlin, Germany, was packed. In one box sat Adolf Hitler. He was the German dictator. Many people in the stands belonged to his Nazi party. It was the only party allowed in the country.

Hitler looked down with cold eyes at a black athlete. The young man was warming up for a short race. Hitler hoped that the black man would lose the race. After all, the dictator had told the world that blacks were not as good as whites. He especially hated Jewish people. In fact, a few years later, he would try to kill all the Jewish people in Europe. He said that white Germans were better than any people on earth. Hitler was certain that the Olympics in Berlin would prove this.

Wide World Photos

Adolf Hitler (first row, second from left) attended many events at the 1936 Olympic Games in Berlin.

But Adolf Hitler could not stop the young black athlete that day. No one could stop him. He won the race by two yards. The loudspeakers rang out, "Winning for the United States—Jesse Owens!"

The time was August 1936. The Olympic Games were taking place. Countries all over the world had sent their best athletes to Germany.

The Olympic Games began more than 2500 years ago in Greece. Those games had lasted for almost 1000 years. Greek athletes came from many countries. The young men could pass through countries at war to go to the games. No country could do them harm.

In the 1890s, Baron Pierre de Coubertin worked hard to get the Olympics started again. The first new Olympic Games began in 1896.

One goal of the great sports meet is to help bring peace to all countries. The Olympics bring together athletes who become friends through the games.

When the Olympics were held in Berlin in 1936, the Nazi ideas were exactly the opposite of everything the Olympics stood for. Hitler wanted the Olympics to show how much better his German athletes were than others. His eyes were angry as Jesse Owens was cheered. Was there no way to stop this popular man?

The next day was the qualifying round for the long jump. To get into the finals, a jumper had to leap 23 feet 5½ inches. Owens had done this many times.

Each jumper had three tries to reach the mark. "Foul!" the judge yelled on Owens's first and second jumps.

The American was sure the judge was wrong. He believed the judge had fouled him to please Hitler. But what could Owens do?

As he stood thinking, he felt a hand on his shoulder. He turned and saw a white athlete dressed in the colors of Germany.

"I'm Lutz Long," said the German, smiling. "I'm glad to meet you, Mr. Owens. I've heard a lot about you."

Owens was puzzled. He knew that Lutz Long was the German team's best jumper. What did he want with him?

"Look, you can jump this in a snap," Lutz Long said, "but that judge is against you. So why not make a mark *before* the take-off board. Then jump from there? There's no way he can disqualify you then."

Now it was Jesse's turn to smile. "A good idea," he said.

He walked down the running path to the take-off board. He turned and took one step back. Then in front of 120,000 people, he made a line in the dirt with his foot. He looked at the German judge and walked back up the path.

Now he ran down the running path, moving easily. With a sudden burst of speed, he came up to the line he had made and

Jesse Owens (center, on victor's stand) is shown here after he was presented the gold medal for winning the long jump competition. Lutz Long is shown standing behind him.

jumped from there. Up, up, up he went. He landed well past the qualifying mark. A roar went up from the people in the stands.

"Thank you," he said to Lutz Long.

That afternoon Jesse Owens won the finals in the long jump. He set an Olympic record. The person in second place was Lutz Long. He would have won if Jesse Owens had been disqualified. Yet the German was the first to hold out his hand when Jesse won.

"It took real courage for him to do that in front of Hitler," Jesse Owens said later about the man who became his friend for life. "It was the finest example of the Olympic spirit!"

APPLYING
READING
SKILLS

A. USING CONTEXT CLUES

Fill in the blanks in this paragraph. Choose from the words below. Use each word only once.

helped	won	Olympics
disqualify	prove	dictator

Adolf Hitler was a cruel German _____. In 1936, Hitler wanted to

_____ that his white German athletes were better than others at the Olympic

Games in Berlin, Germany. But he hadn't counted on a black American named Jesse

Owens. Owens received three gold medals at the _____. In one event, Jesse

Owens was _____ by a German athlete named Lutz Long. A German judge

tried to _____ Jesse in the long jump. But thanks to Lutz's tip, Jesse

_____ the event anyway.

B. SUMMARIZING A STORY

A *summary* is a short statement giving the main points of a story. The paragraph in exercise A is an example of a summary.

Write a summary of "The Olympic Spirit" in your own words. First, reread the story and look for important facts. Then write a short summary (three or four sentences).

C. UNDERSTANDING WORD MEANINGS

Use each of the following words in a sentence. Show by your sentences that you understand the meaning of the words.

1. athlete ....

....

2. puzzled ....

....

3. example ....

....

4. judge ....

....

D. IDENTIFYING ANTONYMS

An *antonym* is a word that is opposite in meaning to another word. *Tall* and *short*, *hot* and *cold*, and *thin* and *fat* are pairs of antonyms.

Put a check (✓) before each pair of antonyms below.

.... 1. walk, run   .... 2. packed, empty

.... 3. look, see   .... 4. win, lose

.... 5. roar, cry   .... 6. talk, speak

.... 7. take, give   .... 8. wish, hope

.... 9. qualify, disqualify   ....10. friend, foe

..........11. stop, halt   ....12. came, went

Write an antonym for each of the following words.

13. sat ....   14. young ....

15. down ....   16. harm ....

17. last ....   18. peace ....

19. stop ....   20. everything ....

21. begin ....   22. lose ....

AERIAL DAREDEVIL

His airplane was made of cloth and wood and wire. But Frank Clarke did tricks with it that no one else could do or wanted to do.

Movie Still Archives

WORDS YOU SHOULD KNOW

Study these words and their meanings before you read the story.

attach—join; fasten to
- The swing was **attached** to the tree with ropes.

cockpit—place in an airplane where the pilot sits
- The **cockpit** of an airplane has all the controls needed to fly the airplane.

controls—things that give power over a machine
- The **controls** of an automobile are in front of the driver's seat.

handcuff—steel bracelets used to keep a person from using his or her hands
- Police officers carry **handcuffs**.

pilot—person who steers an airplane or a ship
- The United States Air Force has many good **pilots**.

stunt—special trick, usually dangerous
- The tightrope walker's best **stunt** was riding a bicycle on the high wire.

People in San Francisco could not believe their eyes that day in 1927. High above San Francisco Bay, 40 airplanes were fighting. They shot and flew at each other. One airplane would miss another by inches.

What was going on? The people could see it was a dogfight—an air battle of airplanes. But there had not been any of those since World War I nine years before. Also, these were not new airplanes. They looked like planes from the war.

"It's a movie," one person said at last. "I can see a person in one airplane taking pictures."

"You could have fooled me," said another. "Looks just like the real thing. They will be lucky if no one gets killed."

No one did get killed that day. But they were not so lucky on other days. Before the movie *Hell's Angels* was finished, three men had died. These fights in the air are still thought of as being the most exciting airplane shots in any movie.

The person who brought all these men together was Frank Clarke. They were all World War I fighters or barnstormers. A barnstormer was a person who did airplane tricks before an audience.

It's been more than 30 years since Frank Clarke flew his last airplane. But stunt people in Hollywood still talk about the things he did. He was the master of them all.

Back in the 1920s, airplanes were very different from those of today. And they were a lot more dangerous. They were made of wood and cloth. Their engines were small. They were

Hatfield History of Aeronautics, Northrop University

Culver Pictures

Hatfield History of Aeronautics, Northrop University

Frank Clarke performed many stunts. Here he is changing planes while in flight.

not fast. Top speed for many of them was 75 miles an hour.

Airplanes were so new that people would turn out from miles around to see them. They would pay good money to see the brave men and women barnstormers do their tricks high in the air.

When he was not making movies, Frank Clarke went barnstorming. One trick the crowds loved to see was wing walking. He would climb out on the upper wing of a two-winged airplane. The pilot in the back cockpit would fly the airplane while Clarke walked, jumped, and danced on the wing. He held a rope that was attached to the wing.

Many barnstormers did this trick. Clarke decided to do it better. During one movie, he played a police officer who was after a crook. He chased the other stunt person all over the wings. One trip and they would have fallen to the ground.

Still, that was not enough. Frank Clarke had himself handcuffed. Then he climbed out on the wing. Even other barnstormers would not do this. It almost ended with him being killed. He tripped as he went back toward the cockpit. He tried to reach for a wire. But he forgot that his hands were bound. He was lucky, though. He fell back against a wire that held the two wings together. He got his balance back and made it to the cockpit.

Some stunt people thought climbing out on the tail of the airplane was even more dangerous. Clarke only laughed at them.

"I'm going to top that," he said. "I'm going up alone. Then I'm going to climb on the tail and fly the airplane."

"How are you going to do that?" asked his friends. They thought he had really gone out of his mind this time.

"I'll have a rope attached to the controls," he answered. "It will be easy."

And it might have been if the rope had not been weak. It snapped while Clarke was sitting on the tail. The small airplane nosed down toward the earth. Faster and faster it went. Clarke held on with his fingers. Slowly, he crawled back to his cockpit. He got there just in time. He pulled the airplane up at the last second before hitting the earth.

Once he had to fly an airplane off a tall city building in a movie. It was not Clarke's idea. The writer of the movie put it in. He didn't really know much about flying.

All of Clarke's friends told him not to do it. The roof was only 95 feet wide. That was very short for a takeoff.

But nothing could stop Frank Clarke. And he made it as hundreds of people in the street cheered. He wagged his airplane's wings at the crowd as he flew down the street.

He was not the first person to go from one airplane to another high in the air. It had been done before with a rope ladder. But that was too easy for Clarke. He wanted to jump from one plane to the other.

He climbed out on a wing. The other airplane was coming close. Then a sudden, hard wind hit Clarke's airplane. His pilot did his best to keep the airplane even. But it jerked anyway. Clarke slipped. His foot went through the wing, and he fell.

For a few moments he was knocked out. When he came to, his pilot waved for him to return to the cockpit. But that was not Frank Clarke's way. If he started a trick, he had to finish.

Even though he was shaking, he got up and walked to the

Hatfield History of Aeronautics, Northrop University

These photos show Clarke buzzing the tower at an airport.

tip of the wing. The other airplane caught up. The wings of the airplanes were very close. Clarke reached out and grabbed the other airplane's wires. Then he swung onto the wing. He had made it.

Not all of Clarke's tricks were done for movies or for barnstorming shows. Once he was dating a singer who worked in a hotel. He found out that her room was on the tenth floor. He wrote her a letter and decided to give it to her himself.

The hotel was at the end of a city street. Clarke's airplane flew very low up the street. At the last moment, he pulled the airplane up. It flew just inches from the hotel's walls. As he passed the singer's room, he threw the letter into the open window.

His greatest trick was one he had not prepared for. A friend named Al Wilson was going to go from one airplane to another—Clarke's great stunt. And Frank Clarke was going to be in the airplane Wilson was jumping to.

Hatfield History of Aeronautics, Northrup University

But something went wrong. As Clarke was bringing his airplane up, Wilson fell off his wing. Without thinking, Clarke dived under his friend and caught Wilson. The falling man hit the upper wing. He stayed there while Frank Clarke brought the airplane safely back to earth.

Frank Clarke's last trick didn't work. He planned to "buzz" a friend who owned a mine in the mountains. When Clarke was over the mine, he started a dive. The plane's controls stuck. Clarke could not pull out of the dive. The plane crashed to the ground and burned. Clarke was killed instantly. It was Friday, June 13, 1948.

APPLYING
READING
SKILLS

A. WRITING A TITLE

Complete the sentence below by writing what you think is the best answer.

Another good title for this story would be ....

....

because ....
....
....
....

B. RECALLING DETAILS

Draw a line under the best ending for each sentence.

1. The airplanes used in the movie *Hell's Angels* were
   a. the very newest kind.
   b. jet fighter planes.
   c. left over from World War I.

2. A barnstormer is a person who
   a. does airplane stunts before an audience.
   b. burns barns for a living.
   c. acts in movies.

3. In the 1920s airplanes were made of
   a. wood and cloth.
   b. plastic.
   c. metal and glass.

4. Frank Clarke was a
   a. war hero.
   b. photographer.
   c. stunt pilot.

5. When his friend Al Wilson fell off an airplane, Clarke
   a. watched Wilson fall to the ground.
   b. flew underneath Wilson and caught him.
   c. threw Wilson a rope, which saved his life.

6. Once, Clarke tried to fly an airplane while sitting on the tail by
   a. controlling it with his feet.
   b. tying a rope to the controls.
   c. locking the controls in place.

7. One of Clarke's best tricks was
   a. walking on an airplane's wing high above the ground.
   b. skydiving from an airplane without a parachute.
   c. flying an airplane upside down.

C. FINDING THE MAIN IDEA

Circle the number of the phrase that best tells what this story is about.

1. Frank Clarke

2. making movies with airplanes

3. barnstorming

4. the early years of flying

D. RECOGNIZING COMPOUND WORDS

When two words are joined, the new word is called a *compound word*. For example, *out* and *side* can be joined to form the compound *outside*.

Some of the words below are compound words. Some are not. If a word is a compound word, write the two words that make it up. Do not write anything if a word is not a compound word.

1. dogfight ....

2. airplane ....

3. finished ....

4. barnstorm ....

5. dangerous ....

6. control ....

7. snapped ....

8. highland ....

9. watchdog ....

10. moment ....

E. DRAWING CONCLUSIONS

Circle the letter of the one answer that best completes each sentence.

1. When three men died while making *Hell's Angels*,
   a. the picture was not successful.
   b. no one would fly for Frank Clarke again.
   c. people knew that movie stunt flying could be dangerous.

2. Frank Clarke
   a. was a reckless pilot.
   b. took unnecessary risks while flying.
   c. was one of the best movie stunt pilots of all.

3. Most of all Frank Clarke liked
   a. flying.
   b. making movies.
   c. scaring his friends with his flying stunts.

4. To be a good movie stunt pilot, a person needs to be
   a. foolish and different.
   b. skillful and daring.
   c. young and strong.

CREATURE AT LOCH NESS

The first written record of a monster in Loch Ness is about 1,400 years old. Thousands of people have reported seeing the monster. Yet, the creature is still a mystery. In fact, many people don't believe there is a Loch Ness monster.

London Daily Express *photograph*, *Pictorial Parade*

WORDS YOU SHOULD KNOW
Study these words and their meanings before you read the story.

camera—machine that takes pictures
- A **camera** is a useful thing to take on a vacation.

creature—any living person or animal
- You are a **creature**.

extinct—no longer existing
- The dinosaur is an **extinct** animal.

imagination—being able to think of new things and ideas
- People who write stories have good **imaginations**.

monster—a strange animal or person
- A two-headed cow is a **monster**.

scientist—person who knows a lot about science
- **Scientists** ask questions about the world around them.

surface—the topmost or outer part of something
- Sometimes, the **surface** of the lake is as smooth as glass.

The night is quiet. The sky is dotted with bright stars. Moonlight spills over the lake. A gentle wind blows over the water.

A man is driving home on the road next to a lake called Loch Ness. He is whistling. He has been visiting friends and has had a good time.

Down, down, down in the lake at the very bottom, the thick mud stirs. The head of a beast slowly rises. It is followed by a huge body.

The creature is shaped like a snake. But is it a snake? It is very long, much longer than a land snake.

It shoots upward. Then it bursts through the surface. Its head is raised high. It turns and looks at the moving car.

The driver does not see the creature at first. But the waves suddenly breaking on the shore catch his eye. He looks toward the lake. His eyes widen. His hands are glued to the wheel.

The car just misses a tree. Then the man pulls the car back onto the road. He steps on the gas.

Five miles on, he speeds into a village. A police officer yells at him, "Stop!"

Wide World Photos

This is one of the most famous photos of the Loch Ness monster. The photographer claims it is the Loch Ness Monster's head, neck, and back. The dark area extending below the neck is a shadow.

The driver slams on his brakes. He sits shaking as the police officer comes up.

"What's your hurry?"

The man's mouth opens. But he cannot speak for a few minutes. At last the words come slowly. "I . . . I . . . saw . . . the monster!"

Back at the lake, the creature stared after the car. Then in a mighty dive, it disappeared back into the water.

Did the man really see a monster? Is there some kind of strange animal living at the bottom of the lovely Loch Ness in Scotland?

Many people who live near the lake think so. For more than 1,400 years, people there have told such tales.

But many scientists don't believe the monster stories. They think people have good imaginations. They sometimes see things that are not really there.

On the other hand, there are scientists who are not quite sure. They say they have open minds about the monster.

London Express *photograph, Pictorial Parade*

This photo shows three humps which are supposed to be part of the monster's back.

London Daily Express *photograph, Pictorial Parade*

Dr. Robert Rines, right, and Sir Peter Scott show a copy of a magazine article which includes an underwater photograph of the monster's head, neck, and part of its body. Dr. Rines headed the expedition which took this photo in 1975.

They point out that once creatures like this really lived. This was before there were men and women on the earth.

That is true, say those who don't believe in the monster. But that creature of long ago lived in the open sea, not in fresh water.

Right, say the scientists who are not quite sure. But once, Loch Ness flowed into the sea. Then dirt filled in and blocked the way to the ocean. Maybe these beasts were trapped in the lake when that happened.

Also, some creatures that were supposed to be extinct have been discovered. A man named Thor Heyerdahl and some friends crossed the Pacific Ocean a few years ago on a raft. One night a strange fish jumped out of the water. It landed on the raft. It was a fish that was believed to have died out a very long time ago.

Robert Rines is one of those who have an open mind. A few years ago he wanted to find the truth. He hired some people to spend a few nights on Loch Ness in two boats.

They had sonar. This is a special machine that picks up sounds from under the water. The sounds make marks on a screen.

One night the sonar screen showed that something large was moving under the water between the two boats. Robert Rines took pictures with an underwater camera.

What do the pictures show? Well, they show what might be a monster. Or it could be just a large shadow. People can't make up their minds.

People living miles and miles from Loch Ness also tell of seeing a lake monster. They have seen it many times in a lake in Siberia. Siberia is part of the Soviet Union. The monster looks like a huge snake. Could this be another Loch Ness monster? What do you think?

Photographers International/Pictorial Parade

This is Loch Ness. Could a monster be living somewhere in its depths?

APPLYING
READING
SKILLS

A. DEFINING WORDS

Study the underlined word in each sentence below. Then draw a circle around the letter of the best definition for that word.

1. The sky is <u>dotted</u> with bright stars.
   a. lightened
   b. rounded
   c. marked

2. The <u>creature</u> is shaped like a snake.
   a. person
   b. lower-type animal
   c. maker

3. Many scientists believe the Loch Ness <u>monster</u> may exist.
   a. cruel person
   b. horrible creature
   c. unusual plant

4. Down in the lake's bottom the thick mud <u>stirs</u>.
   a. moves
   b. thickens
   c. becomes lively

5. The sonar screen <u>showed</u> something.
   a. moved
   b. paraded
   c. revealed

B. UNDERSTANDING MULTIPLE MEANINGS

Many words have more than one meaning. For instance, "land" may mean "ground or soil," "come to ground," "go ashore from a ship," or "catch."

Here are several meanings for the word *break*. Write the letter of the meaning that best fits the way the word *break* is used in each of the following sentences.

a. to pierce
b. a short rest from activity
c. to come apart

.... 1. He saw the creature's head <u>break</u> the surface of the water.

.... 2. After swimming in Loch Ness, they took a short <u>break</u>.

.... 3. If you drop a glass, it will <u>break</u>.

C. ALPHABETIZING WORDS

Put the words in each group in alphabetical order. Look at all the letters in each word before you decide where to put it.

Group One	Group Two	Group Three	Group Four
surface	black	mouth	crossed
slams	beast	minutes	creature
shaking	bursts	minds	catch
speeds	believed	moving	car
sure	behind	monster	could
seen	broke	many	can't

Group One	Group Two	Group Three	Group Four

D. IDENTIFYING FACTS AND OPINIONS

A fact is something that can be proven true. An opinion is what someone thinks. To say that motorcycles are two-wheeled vehicles is a fact. But to say that motorcycles are dangerous is an opinion.

Write *F* in front of each sentence that gives a fact about the story. Write *O* before each sentence that gives an opinion.

.... 1. There is no Loch Ness Monster.

.... 2. The first written record of a monster in Loch Ness is about 1,400 years old.

.... 3. People sometimes see things that aren't there.

.... 4. Some scientists believe that there is a monster in Loch Ness.

.... 5. There used to be creatures similar to the Loch Ness monster.

.... 6. Monsters all died out a long time ago.

.... 7. Loch Ness was once connected to the sea.

.... 8. Robert Rines' sonar pictures show the Loch Ness monster.

THE MYSTERY OF ROOM 342

Mrs. Harvey left the hotel to get some medicine. When she returned, everything had changed. No one knew her. And her sick mother was gone. What had happened? Was she going crazy?

Ketti Kupper

WORDS YOU SHOULD KNOW

Study these words and their meanings before you read the story.

automobile—car
  • After being repainted, the **automobile** looked new again.

bellhop—person in a hotel who carries bags, runs errands, and so on
  • The **bellhop** carried our bags to our hotel room.

clerk—person who checks people in and out of hotels and assigns them their rooms
  • The **clerk** said our room is ready.

elevator—machine for carrying people and things up and down in a building
  • Most tall buildings have **elevators**.

medicine—science of curing diseases or improving health
  • Modern **medicine** has cured many diseases.

plague—very dangerous disease
  • Centuries ago, rats caused many **plagues** in Europe.

Ketti Kupper

The spring of 1900 was a very busy year for Paris, France. A world's fair, the largest up to that time, was about to open. It was hoped that people from all over the world would come to see the many new inventions shown there.

In April, a young English woman and her mother arrived at a small hotel in the city.

"You are so lucky," said the desk clerk. "Our great fair is just opening tomorrow. You will be able to see—"

"I am afraid we will not visit the fair," said the young woman. "We are passing through France on our way to England. We decided to stop here because my mother feels so tired."

The desk clerk looked at the black dress the young woman was wearing. He understood. "You are a widow?" he asked gently.

She nodded. "My husband was in the British army. He was stationed in India. He died a month ago. We are on our way home."

The clerk bowed his head. "I am so sorry. We will do everything to make your stay here a restful one. If you need anything at all, please call on me. My name is Pierre." He turned to a bellhop. "Take Mrs. Harvey's and Mrs. Hall's baggage up to room 342."

The women followed the bellhop into the elevator.

"Poor woman," Pierre said to himself. "So young to have such sadness."

In an hour, Mrs. Harvey came down. "My mother seems to be quite sick," she said to Pierre. "I am very worried. Could you please call a doctor?"

"Certainly, madame," said Pierre. "Do not become excited. A doctor will be here in no time."

Pierre was as good as his word. In ten minutes, a doctor arrived. He looked over the older woman carefully. She was in great pain and barely breathing. The doctor sighed.

"Mrs. Harvey, your mother is indeed very ill," he said. "But I believe I can cure her. I have a special medicine for her. I am the only doctor in Paris who has it. But it is in my office. Would you mind getting it for me?"

"Leave my mother?" cried the widow. "No, I do not—"

Mrs. Hall opened her eyes and smiled. "You go, dear. I will be all right until you return."

"I would go myself," said the doctor. "But I do not think I should leave your mother's side."

"Very well," said Mrs. Harvey. "It seems as if it is the only way."

"Good," said the doctor. "I will go down with you to see that you get a cab."

Outside the hotel, the doctor ran into the street and waved to a cab. It pulled over. The doctor spoke to the driver for a minute. Then he waved for the widow to get in.

"Come, you must hurry," he said. "We have no time to lose."

"It's an automobile," cried Mrs. Harvey. "I won't ride in it. I have never been in one."

"I know automobiles are new," the doctor said. "But believe me, you will be perfectly safe. And it will get you to my office and back quickly."

The young woman felt uneasy, but she got in.

As soon as the automobile had gone around the corner, the doctor went back into the hotel. "Now, here's what I want you to do," he said to Pierre.

Mrs. Harvey returned four hours later. "That driver is the most stupid man I have ever met!" she said excitedly to Pierre. "You would think he knew his way around Paris. But he

Ketti Kupper

Ketti Kupper

kept on losing his way. And on the way back, the automobile broke down. It took him half an hour to fix it. But at least I have the medicine."

Pierre looked at her with a puzzled face. "I am sorry, madame, but I do not know what you are talking about."

"Is everyone in the city losing their mind today?" the young woman cried. "Pierre, I am Mrs. Harvey, my mother is sick, I went to . . . . Oh, never mind."

She started toward the elevator.

"May I ask where you are going?" called Pierre from behind the desk.

"To room 342."

"But why?"

"Because that is my room. That is where my mother is."

Pierre looked up at the ceiling and sighed. "You said your name is Mrs. Harvey?"

"Yes."

"Well, Mrs. Harvey, you can't be in room 342. A Mr. LaRue has had that room for a week."

"Well, maybe I have the number wrong. Which is my room?" Her voice was rising.

"I do not know," he said. "But it is not in this hotel."

She returned to the desk and looked the man in his eyes. "You are Pierre. I am Mrs. Harvey. My mother, Mrs. Hall, and I came to this hotel early this afternoon. You gave us a room."

Pierre shook his head. "I have never seen you before in my life."

"Oh, this is crazy," said Mrs. Harvey. "If you don't stop this, I will call the police."

"As the lady wishes," said Pierre. He waved to the bellhop. "I see a police officer standing just outside the door. Be so good as to call him to step in."

The police officer listened to Mrs. Harvey and Pierre carefully. When they had finished, he said, "You say you have never seen Mrs. Harvey before?"

"Never!"

"Nor you?" he asked the bellhop.

The man shook his head.

"But I tell you I was here!" cried the widow.

"There is only one way to find out," said the officer. "Let us go up to room 342."

The desk clerk held up his hands. "Very well, if that is the only way you see to get rid of her."

"You will see," said Mrs. Harvey to the police officer as the three went up in the elevator.

Pierre knocked on the door of room 342. It was opened by an old man. "What is it?" said the man with a frown. "I am trying to get a little sleep."

The police officer stepped forward.

"I am sorry, Mr. LaRue. But this woman believes this is her room. She says she was given it early this afternoon."

"She must be crazy," said LaRue. "I have been here for a whole week."

"I am not crazy!" said Mrs. Harvey. She brushed past the old man and entered the room. She looked around wildly. "Where is my mother? And where is our baggage? It's different, all different! The furniture—even the wallpaper—has been changed!"

"You must have been mistaken, madame," said the police officer. "It happens with young widows." He pushed her gently out of the room. "Thank you, Mr. LaRue, for your time."

Mrs. Harvey didn't say a word until they were downstairs. Then she remembered. "The doctor! That's it, all we have to do is find the doctor."

"Very well," said the police officer. "His name, please?"

She looked at him with wide eyes. "I don't know."

Ketti Kupper

"Well, where is this office you say you were sent to?"

"I don't know," she whispered. She put her face in her hands and began to cry. "I don't know."

"Let me take you to my station, Mrs. Harvey," the police officer said. He led her toward the door. "We will help you get back to England."

This story has been told again and again. No one knows for sure if it is true. But many people have tried to figure out just what happened.

It is claimed that many years later a very old man named Pierre gave an answer as he was dying.

"The doctor saw right away that Mrs. Harvey's mother had the black plague. What a terrible sickness. She probably got it in India, but it didn't show itself until she reached Paris. There is no cure for it.

"He knew if word of this got out, no one would come to the fair. The government would lose a great deal of money. He sent the widow to his office with a note for his nurse to give her a small bottle of colored water. He told the cab driver to take a great deal of time.

"Then he sent for government officials. They agreed with him. By that time, Mrs. Hall had died. They had her body taken out and buried. Then the room was changed, and Mr. LaRue was put into it. Even the police officer knew what had happened.

"We saved the fair. But, oh, that poor woman! Did I do the right thing, I ask myself again and again. Did I do right?"

APPLYING
READING
SKILLS

A. SUMMARIZING A STORY

Use the words listed below to fill in the blanks and make a summary of the story. Use each word only once.

office	plague	government
medicine	hotel	ill

In 1900, a world's fair opened in Paris. Mrs. Harvey and her mother, Mrs. Hall,

checked into a .... Mrs. Hall became quite ....

The doctor sent Mrs. Harvey to his office to get .... While she was

gone, Mrs. Hall died of the .... The doctor and Pierre moved the

body and changed the room to save the .... a great deal of money.

B. LOCATING WORDS IN A DICTIONARY

In order to use a dictionary well, you need to be able to turn quickly to the part that has the word listed. Think of the dictionary as being divided into three parts. Then you can remember which part to turn to when you look for a word. Here are the three parts.

First Part	**Middle Part**	**Last Part**
a,b,c,d,e,f,g,h,i,j,k	l,m,n,o,p,q	r,s,t,u,v,w,x,y,z

In what part of the dictionary would each of these words be found?

1. busy ....

2. pain ....

3. mother ....

4. quiet ....

5. official ....

6. yellow ....

7. uneasy ....

8. government ....

9. woman ....

10. sleep ....

11. decide ....

12. husband ....

13. colored ....

14. happened ....

15. figure ....

16. widow ....

C. USING DICTIONARY GUIDE WORDS

Most dictionaries have two *guide words* at the top of each page. The guide words help you to find the word you are looking for. The first guide word is the first word on the page. The second guide word is the last word on the page.

The two words printed at the top of each list below are guide words. Put a check (✓) before each word that can be found under the guide words.

undoing—unfriendly	automobile—avid	deny-depth
.... 1. unfit	.... 1. aviary	.... 1. derail
.... 2. unfair	.... 2. automat	.... 2. depend
.... 3. unequal	.... 3. average	.... 3. derby
.... 4. unheard	.... 4. auto	.... 4. den
.... 5. unfasten	.... 5. avert	.... 5. dense

D. UNDERSTANDING CHARACTER TRAITS

Put a check before each expression that tells the kind of person each character was.

Mrs. Harvey	the doctor	Pierre
.... crazy	.... smart	.... lazy
.... loving	.... jealous	.... friendly
.... confused	.... selfish	.... concerned
.... sad	.... tough	.... bossy

E. ORDERING EVENTS

Write *1* before the sentence that tells what happened first in the story. Write *2* before the sentence that tells what happened next, and so on.

.... Mrs. Harvey checked into the hotel with her mother.

.... Mrs. Harvey's husband died.

.... Mrs. Harvey went to the doctor's office to get medicine.

.... Mrs. Harvey's mother died.

.... Mr. LaRue moved into room 342.

RACE AGAINST TIME

The trappers had to travel 1,000 miles through flying snow and ice. The temperature was about 50 degrees below zero. And they had only a short time to get the serum to Nome, Alaska. If the trappers failed, many people would die.

Klamser/AlaskaPhoto

WORDS YOU SHOULD KNOW

Study these words and their meanings before you read the story.

diphtheria—dangerous disease of the throat that is spread by infection
  • Before a cure was found, many people died of **diphtheria**.

hospital—place for the care of the sick or wounded
  • The **hospital** was crowded with people hurt in the fire.

medicine—substance used to cure disease or improve health
  • The sick woman took her **medicine** every morning.

parachute—umbrella-like device used in falling safely through the air from a great height
  • After jumping from his airplane, the pilot opened his **parachute**.

patient—person who is being treated by a doctor
  • The doctor never liked to lose a **patient**.

serum—liquid used to prevent or cure a disease
  • The hospital had a large supply of **serum**.

The young boy was dead. Dr. Curtis Welch hurried from the room. He hated to lose a patient. But he had no time to say even a few words to the parents. He slipped on a heavy fur coat and almost ran down the main street of Nome, Alaska.

A few minutes later, he burst into Mayor George Maynard's office. "George, I have to talk to you."

The mayor shook his head. "Maybe this afternoon, Curtis. I'm too busy this morning."

"Right now!" the doctor snapped. He closed the door and sat by the desk. "Richard Stanley died," he whispered.

"That's too bad," said Maynard. "So young and all that. But I can't do anything about it."

"He died of diphtheria."

The puzzled mayor frowned. "Why are you whispering?"

"Diphtheria is catching. Lord knows how many kids in town will come down with it in the next few days. After that, the adults."

The mayor stood up. "Many people will get sick and die?" he asked in a frightened voice.

"Right!"

Maynard walked up and down the room. "What can we do?"

"There's a serum that can keep people from getting it. I don't have any, though. It will have to be sent here."

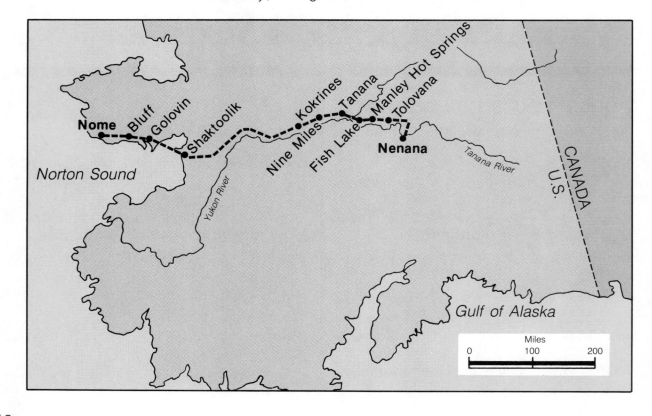

Within five minutes, Maynard was talking by radio to a doctor in the city of Anchorage.

"Sure, we have enough serum for you," the doctor answered. "But it will take a while to get it to Nome. We can get it to Nenana by railroad in a short time. But you know it will take at least two weeks to get it the last 1,000 miles by dogsled."

"Two weeks," Maynard repeated. He looked up at Welch. "That quick enough, doctor?"

The doctor shook his head and said, "A lot of people around here will be dead by that time. But send it anyhow. We will have to do the best we can while we are waiting."

Today, there would be no problem getting medicine to Nome in January. A plane could fly over the ice-locked town and drop the serum by parachute if it could not land.

But Richard Stanley died in 1925. In those days, planes were not able to fly to Nome in such freezing weather and return to their field.

Newspapers told the world that it seemed as if death were going to walk the streets of the small city in Alaska.

But the people in Alaska were tough and didn't give up easily. One of them, a fur trapper named Wild Bill Shannon, slammed his fist on the desk of the sheriff of Nenana.

"That trip can be made in only a few days!" he yelled.

The sheriff shook his head. "Not unless we tie the serum to a reindeer."

"Aw, come on, sheriff. I'm not playing around."

"OK, Bill, just how?"

"By relay teams. Look, there are 15 trading posts between here and Nome. I'll sled to the first post and give the serum to the trapper there. And then that trapper takes off to the next post. And so on and so on."

The sheriff sat back and thought for a moment. "You know, Bill," he said, "I think you have something there."

And so he did. But it was easier said than done. That very day Shannon took off for the first post, Tolovana. In his sled was a metal box with bottles of the serum.

Through the night he whipped his dogs on. The wind blew in his face. It felt like a knife. He could hardly see. But he never thought of stopping.

Dan Green took over at Tolovana right away. It was midnight. He went on to Manley Hot Springs. And so it went from

Courtesy Archives, University of Alaska, Fairbanks

Leonhard Seppala

Manley Hot Springs to Fish Lake to Tanana and on and on. And each driver told the next, "The serum must get through!"

A dogsled had taken off from Nome, too, driven by Leonhard Seppala. Seppala was a fairly young man, but he was known as the best driver in all of Alaska. He did not know that the serum was already on its way. He planned to go all the way to Nenana and return to Nome.

This was to be the hardest drive of his life. It was snowing lightly, but it was enough to freeze his face. He had to brush the snow from his eyes every few minutes so they would not be glued shut. The temperature was about 50 degrees below zero.

Four days later, taking time out only for short naps at trading posts, Seppala met the serum sled. It was only 200 miles back to Nome.

"I'm sure glad to see you, Leonhard," said the other driver. "I have frostbite in my feet. I can hardly step on them."

Taking the serum, Seppala started back toward Nome. After 100 miles he was too weak to go on. But Charlie Olson was waiting. His sled took the life-saving serum the next 70 miles. He turned it over to Gunnar Kaasen.

The light snow turned into a blizzard. Head down, Kaasen kept on. He had to depend on his lead dog, Balto. Balto was

Sam Joseph and his dog team carried the diphtheria serum on one of the legs of the 1,000-mile trip from Nenana to Nome.

Brown Brothers

Gunnar Kaasen and his lead dog, Balto.

Bettmann Archive

Leonhard Seppala and his lead dog, Togo.

half-wolf. He was used to the terrible weather. He and the other dogs pulled on. At last they made it.

The dogs fell in their tracks. A few more miles and they would have died. Kaasen could not get out of the sled. Ice had formed around him. People had to break the ice with hammers.

"Just look at him," said a man when they pulled Kaasen out. "His face is all cut up from the hard snow and wind!"

Dr. Welch didn't wait to see how Kaasen was. He could patch up the driver later. He took the metal box and raced to his little hospital.

"Go tell the mayor we have the serum," he yelled at his assistant. "Have him start lining people up for shots. Hurry. We have no time to waste!"

The trip had taken only six days. The serum had arrived just in time. Because of the brave men who had whipped their dogs through blizzards, only one other person in Nome died of diphtheria.

APPLYING
READING
SKILLS

A. RECALLING DETAILS

Draw a line under the best ending for each sentence.

1. When Dr. Welch lost his patient,

    a. he feared that many people would get sick.

    b. he was very sad.

    c. he gave up medicine.

2. Diphtheria is

    a. a disease that kills all who get it.

    b. an incurable disease.

    c. a disease that is catching.

3. The serum could not be carried by plane because

    a. planes had not been invented.

    b. the weather was too cold.

    c. there were no planes available.

4. Bill Shannon's plan was to

    a. carry the serum by relay teams.

    b. carry the serum by train.

    c. carry the serum by snowmobile.

B. FINDING THE MAIN IDEA

Circle the number of the phrase that tells what the story is mainly about.

1. Richard Stanley
2. getting diphtheria serum to Nome, Alaska
3. dogsledding in Alaska
4. Nome, Alaska

In three or four sentences, explain your choice.

....

....

....

....

C. USING A CONTENTS PAGE

Many books have a *contents* page. You will find it at the front of the book. The contents page tells you the page numbers where things in the book can be found. It also may tell you how the book is organized.

Turn to the contents page of this book. Use it to answer these questions.

1. How many stories are in this book? ....

2. What is the name of Story 3? ....

3. On what page can you find the story called "Aerial Daredevil"? ....

4. On what page does Story 7 begin? ....

5. How many exercises deal with writing a title? ....

6. How many exercises are under "Wheelchair Runner"? ....

D. USING AN INDEX

Many books have an *index*. It is usually located at the back of the book. The words in an index are key words. They are listed in alphabetical order. The page numbers that follow tell you where you can find information about the key word. A key word may have several page numbers after it.

Here is part of an index from a cookbook. Use the index to answer the questions that follow.

New England Clam
   Chowder, 150
Noodles, 82
Nut Cookies, 110
Nut Roll, 192
Old-fashioned Cookies
   Crisp, 296
   Soft, 297
Onion Soup, 164
Onions, 20

Onions, baked, 263
Orange Juice, 203
Orange Sauce, 211
Oysters Rockerfeller, 112
Pancakes, 172
Pancakes, potato, 69
Paprika, 20
Parsley, 21
Pasta, 45, 49, 75, 186
Pastry, 213

Pear Crumb Cake, 98
Pear Tart, 48
Pecan Pie, 187
Peppers, stuffed, 254
Pies:
   Cherry, 232
   Lemon Cream, 233
   Pear Tart, 48
   Pecan, 187
   Pumpkin, 94

1. On what page can you find a recipe for noodles? ....

2. On what page can you find a recipe for potato pancakes? ....

3. On what pages can you find recipes for foods with nuts? ....

4. On what pages can you find recipes for foods with onions? ....

5. On what page can you find a recipe for pumpkin pie? ....

6. How many different pie recipes does the cookbook contain? ....

7. On what page can you find a recipe for stuffed peppers? ....

THEY CALLED HER "TINY"

Her body was small, but her courage was not. Tiny Broadwick was the first woman to jump from an airplane with a parachute.

Movie Still Archives

WORDS YOU SHOULD KNOW

Study these words and their meanings before you read the story.

attach—fasten to
- The mountain climber **attached** a rope to her belt.

harness—straps that fasten a person to something
- The straps on a backpack are a kind of **harness**.

officer—person who commands others in the military
- George Washington was an **officer** in the Continental Army.

parachute—umbrella-like device used in falling safely from a great height
- The sky divers at the air show used brightly-colored **parachutes**.

tangle—to become twisted and knotted together
- Our fishing lines are so **tangled**, we will never get them apart.

There were some people back in 1908 who shook their heads when they heard what Georgia Broadwick planned to do. And she was only 14 years old, too!

Of course, it was all her father's doing, they said. After all, he let her do this . . . this trick of hers. He even backed the young American girl in this silly idea.

They were talking about Georgia's plan to jump from a balloon with a parachute. It was bad enough that some women wanted to be allowed to vote for president, they said. But jumping—well, that was just too dangerous.

Parachutes were nothing new. The first parachute jump had been made in France a few years after the American Revolution. And women had been jumping for a long time—but in Europe. In the United States, it was not thought right for women to do such things.

But Georgia didn't listen to these people. She made her jump in an air show. The people on the ground held their breaths until the parachute opened. Then they clapped loudly.

But the young woman was not going to stop there. It was the first of about 1,100 jumps for her!

Georgia was small. Many people began to call her "Tiny." People soon came to know her as Tiny Broadwick.

Airplanes were very new in those days. On June 21, 1913, Tiny became the first women to jump from one. She didn't leap out, though. The parachute was inside a can that was attached to the side of the airplane. She sat in the parachute harness as if on a swing. Ropes attached the harness to the parachute. When she jumped, the parachute was pulled from the can and opened. She floated softly to the ground.

Tiny also made the world's first planned water jump from an airplane. When making a water jump, the person lands in water. Tiny made her first water jump over Lake Michigan.

In 1914 Charles Broadwick, Tiny's father, designed a smaller and safer parachute. It looked similar to today's parachutes. It was called the Broadwick Safety Pack. It was small enough to be worn on the back of the jumper.

A rope, called a static line, was attached to the parachute pack and the airplane. After a short fall, the rope ripped open the pack. The parachute then opened.

Broadwick wanted the United States Army to try out his new parachute. He was sure that it would save many lives. Finally, army officers agreed to watch how it worked.

National Air and Space Museum, Smithsonian Institution

Tiny's parachute jumps dazzled people who went to watch her at air shows.

Tiny Broadwick, shown here signing a parachutist's log, died on August 25, 1978.

Of course, Tiny was the best person to show it off.

She made her jump in San Diego, California, in 1914. The officers on the ground quietly watched as the airplane went up to about 2,000 feet. Then Tiny jumped.

But something happened that might have killed Tiny. The static line became caught in the airplane's tail. Luckily, she was able to shake the line loose. The parachute opened. She floated safely to the ground.

The army officers were not too sure. It didn't look too safe.

Tiny went back up. And she made history again. She became the first person to open a parachute by hand.

The airplane climbed to about 2,000 feet. Tiny did not attach the static line to the plane. She didn't want to take another chance on the line getting tangled. She looked at the ground for a few moments. Then she jumped out.

After falling about 80 feet, she reached over her shoulder and pulled the static line. The parachute opened. She floated safely to the ground. She had just made the world's first free-fall jump.

Today, many people belong to parachute clubs. These "sky divers," as they call themselves, make free-fall jumps. They owe a lot to the woman who showed the world how it was done.

APPLYING
READING
SKILLS

A. RECALLING DETAILS

Read each sentence. Then write *true* if the sentence is true according to the story. Write *false* if the sentence is not true.

.... 1. Tiny Broadwick was an army officer.

.... 2. Georgia Broadwick's nickname was Tiny.

.... 3. The first parachute jump in the world was made by a woman.

.... 4. Tiny Broadwick got her nickname because of her small size.

.... 5. An early parachute harness looked like a playground swing.

.... 6. A static line keeps a person from falling out of an airplane.

.... 7. Tiny's foster-father helped make a safer parachute.

.... 8. Tiny Broadwick made only about 100 parachute jumps.

.... 9. The first parachute jump in the world was made in France.

.... 10. Today, many parachute jumpers are called "sky divers."

.... 11. Tiny made the first planned water jump from a helicopter.

.... 12. Tiny made the world's first free-fall jump.

.... 13. Parachutes were new at that time.

.... 14. Airplanes were new at that time.

B. ORDERING EVENTS

Write *1* before the sentence that tells what happened first in the story. Write *2* before the sentence that tells what happened next, and so on.

.... Tiny makes the world's first free-fall parachute jump.

.... Tiny parachutes from a balloon.

.... Tiny's foster-father invents a new parachute.

.... Tiny becomes the first woman to parachute from an airplane.

C. ALPHABETIZING WORDS

Put these words in alphabetical order. First find all the words that begin with the letter *a*. Put them in order and write them on the blanks. Then find the words that begin with *b* and so on. Be sure to look at all the letters in each group of words before you decide which word comes first.

depart	insult	did
president	quick	little
victory	retire	women
zero	done	attack

1. ....
2. ....
3. ....
4. ....
5. ....
6. ....
7. ....
8. ....
9. ....
10. ....
11. ....
12. ....

D. ALPHABETIZING TITLES

List the titles below in alphabetical order.

When a title is alphabetized, unimportant words at the beginning of the title are put after the title. These words are *a, an,* and *the*. For example, the title "The Big Dog" would be listed as "Big Dog, The."

"The Power of Song"	"Wheelchair Runner"	"Aerial Daredevil"	"The Olympic Spirit"
"Race Against Time"	"Creature at Loch Ness"	"Superstar"	"Man With a Dream"

1. ....
2. ....
3. ....
4. ....
5. ....
6. ....
7. ....
8. ....

SNOW BIRDS

Skiing is not one sport, but many exciting ones. You can fly like a bird, or go as fast as a car, or race across the countryside.

Wide World/AP Photos

WORDS YOU SHOULD KNOW

Study these words and their meanings before you read the story.

balance—steadiness
- Without good **balance** a skier will fall often.

cross-country—across fields; not by roads
- **Cross-country** skiing is a very popular sport.

ramp—slope
- We moved the car off the truck by using a **ramp**.

skis—pieces of wood or plastic bound one on each foot and used to glide over snow
- Cross-country skiers use different **skis** than downhill skiers.

71

1   There are not many sports I haven't tried. I have played baseball and football. You should see my swimming. I have run in very long races—over 26 miles. And I can play a good game of tennis.

2   But the best sport I have ever tried is skiing. It's fun to watch and much more fun to do. Want to see how exciting it is? Turn on your TV and look at the Winter Olympics or a ski meet.

3   A woman pushes herself away from the top of a high hill. She twists and turns as she goes down. She zips around poles, called gates. She goes faster and faster. She tries to get as near to the poles as she can. But she does not want to knock any down. It is hard to do. She also has to be careful she does not fall. That's hard to do because she is going at such a great speed.

Wide World Photos

Ski jumping is a popular spectator sport in many countries. The jumpers get points based on the length of their jump and their form. The jumper with the most points wins. Good jumpers often leap more than 300 feet.

4   At the bottom of the hill she streaks past the finish line. The clock that has been timing her on her way down stops. The woman waits to hear how fast she has gone. Her time comes over the loudspeaker. Her face falls. She has gone fast, but not fast enough. Three other women went faster.

5   "Too bad," she thinks. "But that was my first run. I still have another try."

6   This race against time in and out of gates is called a slalom. Each racer goes down a hill alone. The fastest time wins.

7   Another exciting event is ski jumping. In this, a skier goes down a very long and steep ramp. The ramp curves up at the end. The skier shoots off the ramp at a very great speed. Higher, higher . . . and still higher the jumper goes. The person's body is stretched out straight like an arrow. Arms are straight down at the jumper's sides.

8   But the jumper is not a bird and must come down sooner or later. The skier drops through the air, almost floating to the ground. The skis hit the snow. Will the jumper be able to keep balance? Or will there be one of those hard and dangerous falls?

9   The landing has been done just right. The skier comes to an easy stop.

10   The jump is measured. 305 feet. It is the longest jump so far. But there are many skiers waiting for their turns. Anyone might beat this distance.

Courtesy Colorado Department
of Public Relations

11   Cross-country racing is not as much fun to watch as jumping. That is because the races are very long. One Olympic race is almost 31 miles. It takes more than two hours. Also, the racers don't do any jumping or downhill skiing.

12   But it is exciting to those in the race. They have to be in top shape to push their way with all their might for such a distance. It looks easy, but it is very hard.

13   My favorite skiing to watch is speed skiing. I have never tried this. There are fewer than 100 high-speed skiers in the world.

14   It is very, very dangerous. The skiers use mountains as their racing courses. The skiers go down alone as fast as they can. They have to bend very low. If the skiers have the wrong form, the wind could break their necks. If the skiers fall, their

suits could catch on fire as they skid along the hard snow.

15 The speed? Up to and over 125 miles per hour! And all on two pieces of thin wood.

16 Racing at high speeds or jumping through the air are only a small part of skiing. This is good because only a few people are able to do those events.

17 But a lot of people like downhill skiing. Try it some time. You have to live in or near a place where there is snow in the winter. If you do not, you can travel to a ski center. Usually, you can find a group going to one on an airplane or bus. It is cheaper to go with a group. You will find ski teachers at the center. They will show you how to put on the skis and move on them. They will start you off on very small hills. When you are good enough, you can try steeper hills.

Cross-country skiing is similar to hiking. Skiers move along snow-covered ground that is flat or slightly hilly.

18 Maybe you don't feel like skiing downhill. Well, you can go skiing through the country. Many people love to spend hours moving as fast or slow as they please through the silent forests and wide, white fields.

19 Whatever kind of skiing you try, I think you will like it. It's been that way since people hundreds and hundreds of years ago picked up pieces of large animal bones. They tied them to their feet and started to move across the snow.

20 That's how skiing was born.

Ben Chesebro/
Tom Stack and
Associates

APPLYING
READING
SKILLS

A. FINDING TOPIC SENTENCES

Each paragraph in a story talks about one idea, or *topic*. Often, that idea will appear in a *topic sentence*. That is, the sentence will tell what the paragraph is about. Every other sentence in the paragraph should relate to that one idea.

A topic sentence may be the first sentence in the paragraph. It may be the last sentence. Or it may appear in the middle of the paragraph.

Write the topic sentence for each paragraph listed below. The first one is done for you.

1. Paragraph 2

   But the best sport I have ever tried is skiing.

2. Paragraph 7

3. Paragraph 12

4. Paragraph 14

5. Paragraph 19

B. ORDERING EVENTS

Write *1* before the sentence that tells what happened first in the story. Write *2* before the sentence that tells what happened next, and so on.

.... The story tells about ski jumping.

.... The story tells about cross-country racing.

.... The story tells about slalom racing.

.... The story tells about speed skiing.

C. MAKING LISTS — CLASSIFYING

Under each heading below, make a list of sports that the story tells about.

Ski Sports	Other Sports
1.	1. ....
2.	2. ....
3.	3. ....
4.	4. ....
5.	5. ....

D. MAKING INFERENCES

Put a check (✓) before each phrase that best completes the following sentence.

Having read the story, it is fair to say that the person telling the story

.... 1. enjoys sports.

.... 2. is easily bored.

.... 3. would rather watch television than ski.

.... 4. is an athlete who has won many medals.

.... 5. loves to ski.

.... 6. likes excitement.

.... 7. is a young person.

.... 8. lives in Colorado.

.... 9. is an Olympic champion.

.... 10. knows a lot about skiing.

.... 11. is proud of his or her sports ability.

.... 12. thinks skiing is an overrated sport.

.... 13. thinks many people would enjoy skiing.

.... 14. is training for the Winter Olympics.

76

THE FREEDOM SINGER

Miriam Makeba had a dream in her heart, a dream of freedom for her people. And she helped them by singing.

Culver Pictures

WORDS YOU SHOULD KNOW

Study these words and their meanings before you read the story.

choir—group of singers
- The Mormon Tabernacle **Choir** is known the world over for its singing.

maid—woman servant
- Being a **maid** is not an easy job.

protect—shield from harm or danger
- Seat belts can **protect** you in an auto accident.

reservation—land set aside for a special purpose
- There are several Indian **reservations** in the United States.

shack—house in bad condition
- Down the street from us is a **shack** that has not been painted in 20 years.

vote—to make a choice in an election
- We will **vote** to select a team captain.

weapon—a thing used for fighting, such as a gun, club, or knife
- The robber did not have a **weapon**.

youth—a young person
- The **youth** of our town need a club.

A young man hurries through the city's dark streets. He looks from side to side. Suddenly, a man steps out of the shadows.

"Show your passbook!" the man orders.

The young man goes through all his pockets. "I . . . I must have lost it," he whispers.

"Lost it!" yells the other man. "And you are not supposed to be here in the city. You are supposed to be back in black town."

"I washed dishes all day," explains the youth. "I did not stop for a rest. At the end, I fell asleep. I just woke up a few minutes ago."

"You don't think I know a lie when I hear it?" said the older man. He flashes a badge. "Police. You are under arrest."

What has the young man done? Nothing! But he has been in the city at night. Only whites can be there after the sun goes down. And he has lost his passbook. Every citizen has to carry a passbook all the time. In it is the whole life story of that person.

Where did this happen? It happened in the country of South Africa. It was in this country that Miriam Makeba was born. Her parents would not have believed that this baby girl would someday become a great singer. How could she? Black people in South Africa were not allowed to do things like that.

In the early 1950's, black people could live in only two places in South Africa. They could live on a kind of reservation. The soil there was very poor. It was hard to make a living.

Or they could live in a black town. This was only a little better than the reservation. The houses were only shacks. There was no electricity. There was no running water. People got sick easily. Many of them died.

And there was no public school. But Miriam Makeba was lucky. She was able to go to a school run by Methodist missionaries. Her teachers found she had a lovely voice. She sang with the choir. This was her first big break.

She married soon after she left school. But the marriage did not last long. Her husband died when she was only 19 years old. She was left with a baby. She did almost the only work black women of South Africa could find. She and her mother worked as maids in the homes of white people in a nearby city.

Every morning Miriam Makeba would leave her shack and

Wide World Photos

take a special bus to the city. She worked all day. The pay was very low. But at least she could feed herself and her child.

She also sang at weddings and parties. But she didn't have much of a life to look forward to. It seemed as if she would always be a maid and live in a shack.

But then a man at a wedding came up to her. "You sing well, Miriam Makeba."

"Thank you," she said.

"I am with a singing group called the Black Manhattan Brothers. There are 11 of us, all men, of course. But now we think we need a woman singer, too. Would you like to join us?"

Would she! She sang with this group for the next three years. It was not easy work. She was either singing or sitting on a bus going to the next place. But she loved it.

Her second big break came when she made some records. They were hits almost overnight.

And her third big break came when she was asked to go to Europe to sing. The government of South Africa did not like this. They made it very hard for her to get permission to leave.

But at last they let her leave. In Europe, people were thrilled by her sweet voice. She sang songs of her people, the Xosa and the Zulu tribes. She also sang songs of other peoples.

Then she came to the United States. She toured the country with a famous singer, Harry Belafonte.

But she never forgot her people in South Africa. She was invited to the United Nations. There she told how blacks were treated in the country of her birth. She told how her proud people lived in shantytowns. She said they were not allowed to own land or vote. Even though four out of five people in South Africa were black, she said, they had no rights at all.

A few weeks later, Miriam Makeba's aunt and three cousins were killed by South African police. In a shantytown called Sharpeville, 20,000 blacks marched peacefully to protest having to carry passbooks. They carried no weapons. They caused no trouble. Suddenly, the police opened fire. Sixty-nine people were killed.

Miriam Makeba hopes to someday return to her country, but only when blacks and whites have the same rights. Until then, she plans to work for the freedom of her people. She does this best, she thinks, through her singing.

Wide World Photos

United Press International

Miriam Makeba

APPLYING
READING
SKILLS

A. RECALLING DETAILS

Find the answers to the questions by looking back at the story. Write your answers in complete sentences on the lines provided.

1. Who is the "freedom singer" in the story?

....

....

2. In what country was the "freedom singer" born?

....

....

3. Where in South Africa could black people live?

....

....

4. Why was Miriam lucky?

....

....

5. How were blacks treated in South Africa?

....

....

6. Who is Harry Belafonte?

....

....

7. What were Miriam's three big breaks?

....

....

....

....

B. ORDERING EVENTS

Write *1* before the sentence that tells what happened first in the story. Write *2* before the sentence that tells what happened next, and so on.

.... Miriam was married.

.... Miriam was asked to sing with the Black Manhattan Brothers.

.... Miriam became a maid.

.... Miriam came to the United States.

.... Miriam spoke before the United Nations.

C. DEFINING WORDS

Write the letter of the best meaning before each word.

.... 1. hurry   a. come apart

.... 2. soil   b. liberty

.... 3. luck   c. move quickly

.... 4. missionary   d. fortune

.... 5. break   e. person who does religious work

.... 6. permission   f. thinking well of yourself

.... 7. shanty   g. cabin

.... 8. weapon   h. dirt

.... 9. proud   i. consent

.........10. freedom   j. gun

D. WRITING A TITLE

Complete the sentence by writing what you think is the best answer.

Another good title for "The Freedom Singer" would be ....

.... because ....

....

"GAME, SET, MATCH"

She was only 13 years old. She was leaving home for the first time. She was going to a tennis school. She had never been to a large city before. Six years later, Evonne Goolagong won the Wimbledon tennis tournament in London.

London Daily Express *photograph*, *Pictorial Parade*

WORDS YOU SHOULD KNOW
Study these words and their meanings before you read the story.

Aborigines—the first people to live in Australia
- When the first settlers arrived in Australia, they found that many **Aborigines** already lived there.

racket—bat used in the game of tennis
- Tennis **rackets** are made of wood, metal, or plastic.

separate—apart
- For years the twins were never **separated**.

tennis—court game played by two or four people using a ball, rackets, and a net
- **Tennis** is a very popular sport in the United States.

tournament—contest among persons in a sport
- The Davis Cup **tournament** is played by the best tennis players in the world.

umpire—person who rules on plays in a game
- The **umpire** called "out!" when she missed the ball on the third strike.

welcome—to greet or receive with pleasure
- When we moved to Memphis, we were **welcomed** by our new neighbors.

Central Press photograph, Pictorial Parade

Central Press photograph, Pictorial Parade

Bill Kurtzman saw the small brown-skinned girl looking through the fence around the tennis court. He thought that he knew all the people in the small town of Barellan, but she was a stranger to him.

"What's your name?" he asked kindly.

"Evonne Goolagong," she answered.

He didn't know it then, but he had just met a child who would become one of the best tennis players in the world. And he was to have an important part in making her a star.

First of all, he had raised the money to have the four tennis courts put up. He had talked to every adult in town to do it. It was not too hard, though. The most popular game in Australia is tennis. In that sunny, warm land, a person can play nearly every day.

Second, he was Evonne's first coach, as he was to all the children in the town. When she was old enough, he asked her if she wanted to play tennis. He knew in the first few minutes that she was much better than any of the others. She had had some practice before that, though. She had spent many, many hours banging a tennis ball against the wall of a garage with an old racket.

Third, he got in touch with Vic Edwards, a top tennis teacher in the city of Sydney. "Mr. Edwards, I'd like to have a six-day tennis school for the children out here in the country. I've got 80 of them who need more help than I can give."

"I can't come myself," said Vic Edwards over the telephone. "I have two teachers working for me, though. If you can raise six dollars a child, I'll send them."

Once again, Bill Kurtzman went to every house in town to get the money. The teachers came. As soon as they saw Evonne running around the court, they were quick to report to Vic Edwards, "One girl here has all the skills to be great."

The teachers came every year. Between their visits, Evonne was winning tournaments in towns around Barellan. Finally, Edwards came to see her play. It did not take him long to see that his teachers were right.

"I think your girl could make a living from tennis," he told Mr. and Mrs. Goolagong. "But I will have to work with her every day. Would you be willing to have her come to Sydney to live with my family?"

Evonne's parents had a large and close family. But they knew this was the girl's big chance. They agreed. And for a

third time Bill Kurtzman went around town for money. He got enough so that the Edwards received six dollars a week for Evonne's food.

Evonne was very nervous when she got on the plane to go to Sydney. All the town was there to see her off. She just hoped she would not let them down.

She was worried about other things, too. She was only 13 years old. That was pretty young for anyone to leave home. Also, she had never been to a city before. What would it be like? In Barellan she knew everyone. Who would be her friends in busy Sydney?

What's more, she was part Aboriginal. She wondered how people would accept that. The Aborigines lived in Australia long before white people came. These natives had not been treated well by the newcomers. Things were getting better for Aborigines, but there were still many white Australians who looked down on them.

She was proud of her Aboriginal background. She wanted to show that her people were as good as anyone else. But still, she was only a child.

She quickly found out that friends were not hard to find in Sydney. She was welcomed by the Edwards as if she were part of the family. There were five daughters. They treated her like a sister.

She roomed with Trisha Edwards, who was her age. They were hardly ever separated. They got along so well that they became doubles partners.

Evonne practiced with Mr. Edwards almost every day after school. A few times a year, she went home to Barellan. She was happy to see her parents and brothers and sisters. But she was also happy to return to Sydney to her "other family."

When she was 19, Vic Edwards decided Evonne was ready to go into big tournaments. And he took her to one of the biggest—the Wimbledon in London, England.

Not many people paid much attention to her. After all, she didn't have a chance to win. She was only a 19-year-old kid. She couldn't beat players like Billie Jean King and Margaret Court.

Evonne surprised everyone by making it all the way to the finals. There she faced a star she worshipped, Margaret Court. Margaret Court was then Australia's top woman star. Evonne had played her in a number of tournaments in Australia. She had won the last time. But that might have been luck. Maybe Margaret Court had had a bad day. Wimbledon was different. There everyone played their best. And Margaret Court had won the year before.

It was a long, well-played match.

In the stands, Vic Edwards sat, biting his nails. "Watch your forehand, Evonne," he was saying silently. "Put more spin on your serve." But of course, she didn't hear him.

Back in Barellan, the whole town watched the match on TV. "Come on, Moochie," they yelled. It had been her nickname since she was a baby.

At last the umpire announced, "Game, set, and match to Evonne Goolagong." She had won the tournament.

The crowd broke into long and loud cheers.

Wide World/AP Photos

A. IDENTIFYING FACTS AND OPINIONS

Write *F* in front of each sentence that gives a fact about the story. Write *O* before each sentence that is an opinion.

.... 1. Evonne Goolagong is part Aboriginal.

.... 2. Evonne's first tennis coach was Bill Kurtzman.

.... 3. Vic Edwards is the best tennis coach in Australia.

.... 4. Evonne became a successful tennis star because her parents let her play the game whenever she wanted to.

.... 5. Evonne's parents wanted her to succeed in tennis.

.... 6. When Evonne left home for Sydney, she was 13 years old.

.... 7. Aborigines were the first people to live in Australia.

.... 8. Australians are the best tennis players in the world.

.... 9. Evonne Goolagong is the best tennis player in the world.

..........10. Tennis is a more exciting game to play than American football.

B. UNDERSTANDING MULTIPLE MEANINGS

Many words have more than one meaning. For instance, *land* may mean "ground or soil," "to come to ground," "to go ashore from a ship," or "to catch."

Here are several meanings for the word *kind*. Write the letter of the meaning that best fits the way the word *kind* is used in each of the following sentences.

a. friendly
b. sort or variety
c. natural group

.... 1. I like many <u>kinds</u> of ice cream.

.... 2. A <u>kind</u> person tries to help people.

.... 3. Our zoo has all <u>kinds</u> of animals.

Here are several meanings for the word *court*. **Write the letter of the meaning that best fits the way the word** *court* **is used in each of the following sentences.**

a. place marked off for a game
b. short street
c. seek to marry
d. place where justice is given out
e. try to get

.... 4. We live on Lincoln Court, which is just off Main Street.

.... 5. Auto race car drivers often court danger.

.... 6. The court found her guilty of murder.

.... 7. Our basketball court now has lights.

.... 8. My father courted my mother all through high school.

Here are several meanings for the word *raise*. **Write the letter of the meaning that best fits the way the word** *raise* **is used in each of the following sentences.**

a. lift up
b. make higher
c. to collect
d. say in a loud voice

.... 9. When we heard there would be no school, we raised a loud shout.

.... 10. Every day it seems that the price of food is being raised.

.... 11. Raise your hand if you have a question.

.... 12. The band members are trying to raise money for their trip to the Rose Bowl parade.

Here are several meanings for the word *play*. **Write the letter of the meaning that best fits the way the word** *play* **is used in each of the following sentences.**

a. to do in fun
b. act or move in a game
c. move quickly or lightly
d. do foolish things

.... 13. The moonlight played on the calm ocean.

.... 14. Somebody played a joke on me.

.... 15. Terry made a good play at second base.

.... 16. Don't play with your life; you only have one.

88

FINAL
REVIEW

A. FINDING THE MAIN IDEA

Read the following paragraph. Then draw a circle around the letter of the answer that best completes the statement.

Most people visit Yellowstone National Park in the summer. But I think the best time to go is in the winter. Then the tourists are gone. I feel as if the whole park is mine. And then everything is covered with snow. Heat and steam from the geysers give the landscape a ghostly look. All roads except one are closed. Cross-country skiers can travel over the trails through the park. Often a ranger will show you where to see the animals feeding. You may even get to feed some deer yourself! Yes, winter in Yellowstone is a very special time.

The main idea of this paragraph is:

a. Many people visit Yellowstone National Park in the summer.
b. In the wintertime, the landscape has a ghostly look.
c. Winter in Yellowstone is a special time.

B. RECALLING DETAILS

Read the above paragraph again. Then draw a circle around the letter of the answer that best completes each statement.

1. In winter, all roads
   a. are closed.
   b. have to be plowed.
   c. are closed, except for one.

2. Cross-country skiers
   a. can feed the bears.
   b. travel over the trails.
   c. help clear the snow.

3. Most tourists like to visit Yellowstone in the
   a. summer.
   b. fall.
   c. winter.

4. In winter, rangers
   a. often are available as guides.
   b. spend all their time feeding the animals.
   c. go on vacation.

C. IDENTIFYING SYNONYMS AND ANTONYMS

Write *S* before each pair of synonyms. Write *A* before each pair of antonyms.

1. .... disease, plague   6. .... form, shape

2. .... extinct, living   7. .... build, destroy

3. .... creature, animal   8. .... forward, backward

4. .... friend, enemy   9. .... center, middle

5. .... scared, afraid   10. .... synonym, antonym

D. DEFINING WORDS

Write the letter of the best meaning before each word.

1. .... obstacle   a. liquid used to control disease

2. .... chaplain   b. a long footrace

3. .... patrol   c. something in the way to overcome

4. .... penalty   d. a ruler with complete power

5. .... marathon   e. a religious leader in a large group

6. .... dictator   f. a very dangerous disease

7. .... stunt   g. a special dangerous trick

8. .... plague   h. apart

9. .... serum   i. traveling an area to guard it

10. .... separate   j. punishment

E. ALPHABETIZING WORDS

Arrange these words in alphabetical order.

injury   attack   robbery   explosion   deliver
beautiful   invention   professional   hospital   tournament

1. ....   6. ....

2. ....   7. ....

3. ....   8. ....

4. ....   9. ....

5. ....   10. ....

ANSWER KEY

STORY 1 (pp. 4-5)
A. 3 **B.** 1. b; 2. c; 3. a; 4. c; 5. c **C.** 1. weary; 2. completed; 3. disliked; 4. bed; 5. afraid **D.** 1, 3, 4, and 7 are antonyms

STORY 2 (pp. 9-10)
A. 4 **B.** 1. true; 2. false; 3. false; 4. false; 5. false; 6. true; 7. true; 8. true; 9. false; 10. false; 11. false; 12. true **C.** 1. began; 2. remain; 3. perform; 4. bashful; 5. poor; 6. ladies; 7. untamed; 8. quick; 9. ocean; 10. pleasant; 11. quiet; 12. song; 13. unusual; 14. watching; 15. shouted; 16. unhappy **D.** 1, 4, 8, 9, 10, 12, 13, 15, 17 are antonyms

STORY 3 (pp. 14-15)
A. 1. a; 2. c; 3. b; 4. a; 5. b; 6. a; 7. a **B.** 2; 1. c; 2. b **C.** 1. goal; 2. have; 3. training; 4. difficult; 5. began

STORY 4 (pp. 19-20)
A. 1. c; 2. a; 3. a; 4. b; 5. a; 6. b **B.** 1 **C.** 1. d; 2. a; 3. f; 4. h; 5. c; 6. g; 7. b; 8. e **D.** The Coast Guard gave Beverly Kelley a desk job because she was a woman. She began writing to Coast Guard headquarters, asking to go to sea. Her determination paid off. She finally gained command of a ship called the Cape Newagen.

STORY 5 (pp. 24-25)
A. 1. true; 2. false; 3. false; 4. true; 5. false; 6. true; 7. true; 8. false; 9. false; 10. true **B.** 1. sports writer; 2. touch down; 4. foot ball; 5. pick up; 6. drop kick; 8. base ball; 10. basket ball; 12. kick off **C.** 1. twist; 2. ruin; 3. believe; 4. turn; 5. marine; 6. palace; 7. forgot; 8. near; 9. gold; 10. pour; 11. roar; 12. build; 13. swim; 14. great

STORY 6 (pp. 29-30)
A. 1. d; 2. e; 3. g; 4. b; 5. f; 6. c; 7. h; 8. a **B.** 2 **C.** Answers will vary. Some examples are 1. a lasting injury or a physical or emotional problem someone was born with. 2. she is his sister. 3. he is afraid that people will laugh at him. 4. the other runners wanted Martin to race. **D.** Martin was a star in soccer, basketball, and baseball. Then he was injured in an automobile accident. He had to use a wheelchair to get around. But Martin could not give up being a sports star. He began training for the city marathon. At first, the judges would not let a person in a wheelchair run the marathon. But the other runners yelled until the judges changed their minds. Martin finished the race, number 20 in a field of 200. **E.** Answers will vary.

STORY 7 (pp. 35-36)
A. Adolf Hitler was a cruel German dictator. In 1936, Hitler wanted to prove that his white German athletes were better than others at the Olympic Games in Berlin, Germany. But he hadn't counted on a black American named Jesse Owens. Owens received three gold medals at the Olympics. In one event Jesse Owens was helped by a German athlete named Lutz Long. A German judge tried to disqualify Jesse in the long jump. But thanks to Lutz's tip, Jesse won the event, anyway. **B.** Answers will vary. **C.** Answers will vary. **D.** 1. 2, 4, 7, 9, 10, and 12 are antonyms; 13. stood; 14. old; 15. up; 16. help; 17. first; 18. war; 19. go; 20. nothing; 21. end; 22. win

STORY 8 (pp. 41-43)
A. Answers will vary. **B.** 1. c; 2. a; 3. a; 4. c; 5. b; 6. b; 7. a **C.** 1 **D.** 1. dog fight; 2. air plane; 4. barn storm; 8. high land; 9. watch dog **E.** 1. c; 2. c; 3. a; 4. b

STORY 9 (pp. 49-50)
A. 1. c; 2. b; 3. b; 4. a; 5. c **B.** 1. a; 2. b; 3. c **C.** Group 1: seen, shaking, slams, speeds, sure, surface; Group 2: beast, behind, believed, black, broke, bursts; Group 3: many, minds, minutes, monster, mouth, moving; Group 4: can't, car, catch, could, creature, crossed **D.** 1. O; 2. F; 3. F; 4. F; 5. F; 6. O; 7. F; 8. 0

STORY 10 (pp. 57-58)
A. In 1900, a world's fair opened in Paris. Mrs. Harvey and her mother, Mrs. Hall, checked into a hotel. Mrs. Hall became quite

ill. The doctor sent Mrs. Harvey to his office to get <u>medicine</u>. While she was gone, Mrs. Hall died of the <u>plague</u>. The doctor and Pierre moved the body and changed the room to save the <u>government</u> a great deal of money. **B.** 1. first; 2. middle; 3. middle; 4. middle; 5. middle; 6. last; 7. last; 8. first; 9. last; 10. last; 11. first; 12. first; 13. first; 14. first; 15. first; 16. last **C.** Under **undoing-unfriendly**--1; 2; 3; 5. Under **automobile-avid**--1; 3; 5. Under **deny-depth**--2 **D.** Under **Mrs. Harvey**--loving, confused, sad. Under **the doctor**--smart, tough. Under **Pierre**--friendly, concerned **E.** 2, 1, 3, 4, 5

STORY 11 (pp. 64-65)

A. 1. a; 2. c; 3. c; 4. a **B.** 2. Answers will vary. **C.** 1. 15; 2. "Man With a Dream"; 3. 37; 4. 31; 5. 2; 6. 5 **D.** 1. 82; 2. 69; 3. 110, 192 (187 may also be considered.); 4. 164, 20, 263; 5. 94; 6. 5; 7. 254

STORY 12 (pp. 69-70)

A. 1. false; 2. true; 3. false; 4. true; 5. true; 6. false; 7. true; 8. false; 9. true; 10. true; 11. false; 12. true; 13. false; 14. true **B.** 4, 1, 3, 2 **C.** attack, depart, did, done, insult, little, president, quick, retire, victory, women, zero **D.** 1. "Aerial Daredevil"; 2. "Creature at Loch Ness"; 3. "Man With a Dream"; 4. "The Olympic Spirit"; 5. "The Power of Song"; 6. "Race Against Time"; 7. "Superstar"; 8. "Wheelchair Runner"

STORY 13 (pp. 75-76)

A. 1. done; 2. Another exciting event is ski jumping. 3. It looks easy, but it is very hard. 4. It is very, very dangerous. 5. Whatever kind of skiing you try, I think you will like it. **B.** 2, 3, 1, 4 **C.** Under **Ski Sports**--1. slalom; 2. ski jumping; 3. cross-country; 4. high speed skiing; 5. downhill racing. Under **Other Sports**--1. baseball; 2. football; 3. swimming; 4. running; 5. tennis **D.** 1, 5, 6, 10, 11, 13

STORY 14 (pp. 81-82)

A. Answers will vary. Some examples are 1. Miriam Makeba is the freedom singer. 2. She was born in South Africa. 3. They could live on a kind of reservation or in a black town. 4. Miriam was able to go to a missionary school. 5. They had to carry passbooks, they lived in shacks, and they didn't make much money. 6. He is a famous singer. 7. She got to sing in the choir. She made some hit records. She was asked to go to Europe to sing. **B.** 1, 3, 2, 4, 5 **C.** 1. c; 2. h; 3. d; 4. e; 5. a; 6. i; 7. g; 8. j; 9. f; 10. b **D.** Answers will vary.

STORY 15 (pp. 87-88)

A. 1. F; 2. F; 3. O; 4. O; 5. F; 6. F; 7. F; 8. O; 9. O; 10; O **B.** 1. b; 2. a; 3. c; 4. b; 5. e; 6. d; 7. a; 8. c; 9. d; 10. b; 11. a; 12. c; 13. c; 14. a; 15. b; 16. d

FINAL REVIEW (pp. 89-90)

A. c **B.** 1. c; 2. b; 3. a; 4. a **C.** 1. S; 2. A; 3. S; 4. A; 5. S; 6. S; 7. A; 8. A; 9. S; 10. A **D.** 1. c; 2. e; 3. i; 4. j; 5. b; 6. d; 7. g; 8. f; 9. a; 10. h **E.** 1. attack; 2. beautiful; 3. deliver; 4. explosions; 5. hospital; 6. injury; 7. invention; 8. professional; 9. robbery; 10. tournament